7 Churches . . .

and their Report Cards

William H. Jones

7 Churches . . .

and their Report Cards

William H. Jones
ChiRho Communications

7 Churches . . .

and their Report Cards

William H. Jones

ChiRho Communications ☧
William H. Jones.
Copyright © 2011 All rights reserved.
Front **Cover: Ephesus Great Theatre**

photo *by* **William H. Jones**
wmhjones9@gmail.com

ISBN 978-0-929081-27-4

Behind the writing . . .

Many are those who have read and mis-read the Apocalypse of *Revelation*. This writer has also been fascinated not only with the book, but especially the first three chapters which detail the Lord's Report Card to the Seven Churches. They represent all other churches of God's communities within the scope of God's all-seeing, evaluating eyes.

Marshall and Hazel Thompson, at one time "friendship workers" in Turkey, first introduced me physically to the "Seven." Since then, I have "taught" courses on the Seven Churches of Asia Minor, and returned a few years later with a CTV Toronto (then called CFTO) video camera crew to create some six documentary programs for Canadian television. Bill Burrows was the director/producer. Other presenters than me (Baptist) in the series titled, *The Kingdom and the Empire* were Fr. John Newton (Roman Catholic); Fr. Jim Collins (Anglican); Rev. Dr. Gordon Fish (Presbyterian); Rev. Earl Albrecht (Lutheran); and Rev. Harold Burgess (United Church of Canada). This book encompasses a much more detailed study than did the TV documentary.

I have been equally fascinated by the island of Patmos. The TV crew did not go there. Patmos has been a welcome retreat for me on several occasions when I wanted short and tranquil respites. Among the engaging Greek Islands, Patmos is probably much less visited. Its population is relatively small. It has no airfield. Its rooms-for-rent are moderately priced. Patmos places one in the milieu where the writer John was visited by his Lord to write a report card on the Lord's churches and to set in motion the mysterious coded representations described throughout *Revelation*.

Some archaeological remains, with an iron work fence around them, near the waterfront of the main town, suggest an added detail. Monks on the island claim the ruins represent a basilica that dates to the time of John. I doubt that can be proven.

It is my hope and prayer that through this book some of the mysteries of the first three chapters of the Apocalypse will be decoded sufficiently to make sense to the reader.

Table of Contents

INTRODUCTION 9

CHAPTER ONE
PATMOS 21

CHAPTER TWO
EPHESUS...41

CHAPTER THREE
SMYRNA..55

CHAPTER FOUR
PERGAMUM...67

CHAPTER FIVE
THYATIRA...79

CHAPTER SIX
SARDIS..93

CHAPTER SEVEN
PHILADELPHIA 107

CHAPTER EIGHT
LAODICEA 121

CHAPTER NINE
EPILOGUE 141

INTRODUCTION

The world in which John penned *The Revelation of Jesus Christ* was topsy-turvy. The date of writing, somewhere before the turn of the first century, put the scene in a context of severe Christian persecution. John himself claimed no authorship. He wrote that, *"God gave him* [the revelation] to show his *servants what must soon take place"* (1:1).

The Christian faith was blossoming rapidly. Its growth agenda bothered Roman officialdom because the citizens of this swelling segment of Roman society irritated the emperor. It troubled previous emperors like Nero but Caligula was especially upset by believers who claimed "Jesus is Lord." Was not Caligula lord? He thought so. Having citizens dismiss the divine emperor cult so easily was a threat to Roman authority – or so the emperor believed.

The book of *Revelation* is more correctly titled *The Revelation of Jesus Christ*. Its purpose is to reveal the Saviour and Lord in the fullness of his glory, power, judgment, and sovereignty. The book begins with Jesus commenting on his Church and churches. The book ends with a vision of his ultimate place at the end of time and history. It is a book about victory, triumph and success. Evil has been defeated. Death has been vanquished. *Revelation* instructs believers about their expected exaltation and the exultation of King Jesus. We realize this admonition is set in the conflicted times of mad emperors. They thought themselves to be gods. They expected every subject to bow the knee to their divinity.

The people who have been redeemed are now in God's complete care and comfort. They are at worship as they should be, mingled in union before him in total praise. These saved and sanctified saints are unhindered by their past sins or their present cares. Their trials, agonies, illnesses, losses have passed into oblivion. They have been judged by God, represented by Jesus the mediator and acquitted. They have been admitted fully into the presence of God. Now they have opportunity to praise him and revel in his beauty as they mingle in the company of the enthroned Jesus, glorified and honoured by the Father.

The first three chapters of this fascinating book of *Revelation* represent the exalted Lord Jesus and his beloved Church, his "bride." This assemblage standing before the Creator of heaven and earth is the Body of Christ, the collection of Jesus' grace-trophies of those whose sins were nailed to the cross of Jesus. They stand responsibly before him to account for their stewardship. Any who hold to an easy and cheap grace, as Dietrich Bonheoffer called it, or a placid faith that requires no accountability, will avoid these three biblical chapters. Our schoolwork is graded by our teachers. Our efforts to please God are marked by the Master. Why should we expect otherwise? We never deserve God's grace; it is a gift from our "gracious" Sovereign. Yet we must answer for accepting it.

Response-Ability

Even those who trust that God has forgiven their omissions and commissions must honestly face the Judge Eternal enthroned in splendour. He will judge them. He will make known their failed responsibilities, not only to them, but to all the glorified saints. Our guilt and our absolution will be a public matter for all the Church to hear, a divine decree from the Everlasting Judge. Each church standing among the seven churches knows the strengths and failings of all other six churches. Before God, all secrets are known and all attitudes exposed. Nothing is hidden from the One who is Alpha and Omega, the beginning and the end, the first and the last.

If this fact surprises anyone, check the record. God knows every detail of our existence. First, it is Jesus' Church. *I will build my church*, said the Lord (Matthew 16:18). The architect has a right to transparency from workmen and women who contract out for him. At the border, all who return from another country must declare what they have brought back from abroad. Jesus spoke to his disciples about their responsibilities and compared the Kingdom of God to a businessman going abroad and delegating responsibilities to his employees. "What are you declaring?" he asks.

11

"It is like a man going on a trip who called his servants and turned his money over to them. To one man he gave five talents, to another two, and to another one, based on their ability. Then he went on his trip.

"The one who received five talents went out at once and invested them and earned five more. In the same way, the one who had two talents earned two more. But the one who received one talent went off, dug a hole in the ground, and hid his master's money.

"After a long time the master of those servants returned and settled accounts with them. The one who had received five talents came up and brought five more talents, saying, 'Master, you gave me five talents. See, I've earned five more talents.' His master said to him, 'Well done, good and trustworthy servant! Since you have been trustworthy with a small amount, I will put you in charge of a large amount. Come and share your master's joy!'

"The one with two talents also came forward and said, 'Master, you gave me two talents. See, I've earned two more talents.' His master said to him, 'Well done, good and trustworthy servant! Since you have been trustworthy with a small amount, I will put you in charge of a large amount. Come and share your master's joy!'

"Then the one who had received one talent came forward and said, 'Master, I knew that you were a hard man, harvesting where you haven't planted and gathering where you haven't scattered any seed. Being afraid, I went off and hid your talent in the ground. Here, take what is yours!'

"His master answered him, 'You evil and lazy servant! So you knew that I harvested where I haven't planted and gathered where I haven't scattered any seed? Then you should have invested my money with the bankers. When I returned, I would have received my money back with interest. Take the talent from him and give it to the man who has the ten talents. For to everyone who has something, more will be given, and he will have more than enough. But from the person who has nothing, even what he has will be taken away from him. Throw this useless servant into the outer darkness! In that place there will be weeping and gnashing of teeth'" (Luke 19:11–30 NIV).

Does the reader miss the point? God expects our accountability. He trusted us with his gospel and we accepted that when we joined him in faith. Did we not realize that we are in partnership with Jesus in every detail of our existence? The Holy Spirit gifted the church with specific people to carry out Jesus' ministry assignments. What have the recipients of these gifts done with them?

He gifted some to be apostles, others to be prophets, others to be evangelists, and still others to be pastors and teachers, to perfect the saints, to do the work of ministry, and to build up the body of Christ until all of us are united in the faith and in the full knowledge of God's Son, and until we attain mature adulthood and the full standard of development in Christ (Ephesians 4:11–13 NIV).

These people are accountable and answerable to the charge God gave them. God can and will forgive their failings if they have not carried out their assignments. God wants them to know what they have done to miscarry his apostolate. God holds all believers liable not only for their deeds but also for their words. *"I tell you,"* said Jesus, *"on the day of judgment people will give an account for every thoughtless word they utter. For by your words you will be acquitted, and by your words you will be condemned"* (Matthew 12:36–37). The last book of the Bible reinforces the answerability of every citizen of God's wide commonwealth.

Yes, God watches us. "He sees the little sparrow fall; it meets his tender view," as the children's song says. Jesus told us that God knows every bloom in his garden, every songbird in his sky, and every garment we wear. He also knows our bank balance, our wardrobe and our opinions about his world. He knows us and understands us. He loves us. And when we say we love him, he expects that our love for him will bear good fruit. *"But if anyone obeys his word, God's love is truly made complete in him. This is how we know we are in him: Whoever claims to live in him must walk as Jesus did"* (1 John 2:5–6).

> *"Therefore I tell you, do not worry about your life, what you will eat or drink; or about your body, what you will wear. Is not life more important than food, and the body more important than clothes? Look at the birds of the air; they do not sow or reap or store away in barns, and yet your heavenly Father feeds them. Are you not much more valuable than they? Who of you by worrying can add a single hour to his life?*
> *"And why do you worry about clothes? See how the lilies of the field grow. They do not labor or spin. Yet I tell you that not even Solomon in all his splendor was dressed like one of these. If that is how God clothes the grass of the field, which is here today and tomorrow is thrown into the fire, will he not*

much more clothe you, O you of little faith?
(Matthew 5:25–31).

God watches every penny we spend and every cent we give away. *"Jesus sat down opposite the place where the offerings were put and watched the crowd putting their money into the temple treasury. Many rich people threw in their large amounts. But a poor widow put in two very small copper coins, worth only a fraction of a penny"* (Mark 12:41–42).

Notice the verbs describing how the donors made their offerings. The rich *threw* in their offerings like tokens in a highway tollbooth. They treated this matter like an obligatory tax. The lowly lady lightly *laid* her offering in the Temple receptacle. She respected her gift and she knew its purpose. God not only watches what we do but he perceives the attitudes with which we esteem his enterprises.

God also knows us – intimately. *"He knows how we were formed,"* wrote the psalmist. *"He remembers that we are dust"* (Psalm 103:14). He also understands why we act the way we do. *"Show me. O LORD, my life's end,"* the poet wrote elsewhere, *"and the number of my days; let me know"* (*"how frail I am"* [KJV] *"how fleeting is my life"* [NIV] Psalm 39:4). Fortunately, God knows all about human frailty. We need never fear punishment under his merciful judgment of our accountability. God is not a bully. He will not terrorize us. Yet he insists that we answer for the life he has given to us and the tasks he has assigned to us.

For sure, God loves us. God loves us "big time." Parents discipline their children, partly so that the kids will not repeat the same mistakes. While the children may not understand their parents' love, the parents issue discipline out of love for their offspring. A parent knows what is better for them than they can understand at their tender age. In eternity, no one will repeat the same mistakes. Yet love demands that we hear the charges God lays against us. Love also demands that God's forgiving, merciful love, respond in us the way a loving parent would. "Son, I love you." "Daughter, I love you." "You messed up, but I want to be your friend and companion forever," God proposes. Then God will hand out his rewards for what we did right!

Decodifying *Revelation*

Revelation is thoroughly coded. To decipher some of the narrative, the reader must learn the biblical enigma code. As one reads through the Apocalypse, one quickly discovers the variety of puzzles embedded in the document. This is a challenge. Some codes are animal codes. Some are numerical codes. Some are colour codes. If one can press the "reveal codes" button on the biblical template, one can find some vital meaning to the text. This book does not inspect the meaning of these many encryptions, only the numerical codes embedded in the first three chapters of this document.

Why the number Seven? The *Revelation of Jesus Christ* uses a number to describe the Body of Christ. The number is seven. In biblical parlance, seven is a complete number. It comprises the number of earth (four) with the number of heaven (three) to total seven. Seven is a recurring theme throughout the Bible. Creation represents six plus one days, a total of seven. This signifies completion of creation.

So, in the fuller scripture text of *Revelation*, we read of seven churches, seven visions, seven seals, seven trumpets and seven bowls. Seven is significant. New Testament scholar James L. Blevins sees the book as drama (*Revelation as Drama*) in which the story is played out on the Ephesian theatre's great stage in seven acts with seven scenes in each act. *Revelation* is about prophesy (forth-telling), the winding up of the Genesis story in which God created humankind, only to result in a broken fellowship with him. But now the story concludes. John's vision articulates how humankind had been once more admitted into fellowship with God through the atonement of Jesus Christ. It summarizes the end of history and is more glorious than the beginning. It is the "wrap" on God's achievements, all symbolized in its completion by the word "seven."

Leaf through the Bible and realize how coded it is. In entering the land promised to them, the Israelites led by Joshua marched around Jericho for seven days (Joshua 3). Their warfare in that place was completed and done with on Day Seven. Naaman, army commander of the king of Aram became leprous. When he visited Elisha, the man of God told him to wash in the Jordan River seven times. When Naaman followed instructions, his healing was absolute (2 Kings 5). When Peter asked Jesus how many times he should forgive someone, say seven times? Jesus answered, "seventy-seven" times (Matthew 18:22). Forgiveness must be absolutely complete. Jesus told of a vacuum in the life of a person whose evil spirit was dislodged but in the void, seven more evil spirits chose to inhabit that individual (Luke 11:26). That amounted to absolute anarchy.

The first three chapters of *The Revelation of Jesus Christ* expose the assets and liabilities of the Seven Churches of Asia Minor. Obviously, more than seven churches had been established throughout the Roman Empire. Seven represents the complete church, all the churches everywhere,

17

whose accountability is illustrated by the individual churches of Ephesus, Smyrna, Pergamum, Thyatira, Sardis, Philadelphia and Laodicea. For that matter, there were churches nearby Laodicea, such as Hierapolis and Colossae.

To underline the completeness in this imagery of the Seven Churches, note that geographically, they form a very rough circle. Look on the map and draw lines between the named churches and they suggest a "circle of seven." Such imagery implies completeness. John knew this territory well. Likely, he knew all about the mentioned churches. He knew their strengths and weaknesses, their accomplishments and failures. John is touted in "tradition" as having been a leader in the Ephesian church, and by that same tradition domiciled in Ephesus.

Today, a house on the outskirts of that city boasts a residence venerated as the abode of Mary, mother of our Lord. John, the rumour proposed, provided the house for Mary based on Jesus' words from the cross, *"Dear Mother, here is your son"* . . . *"Son, here is your mother."* (John 20:26–27).

This book makes no pretense in explaining all the chapters of *Revelation*. It deals only with the first three chapters of a very complicated book. It is a coded writing. The codes were best understood by those in the real time of the earliest churches. We can, however, extrapolate the issues of the past and apply them to the church of modern times. It is a big job to do and a very important task for all believers. It zooms in to the issues facing the Church in the past and equally so in modern times to stress the importance of the Church's answerability and individual accountability to God.

Seven Churches Plus Patmos

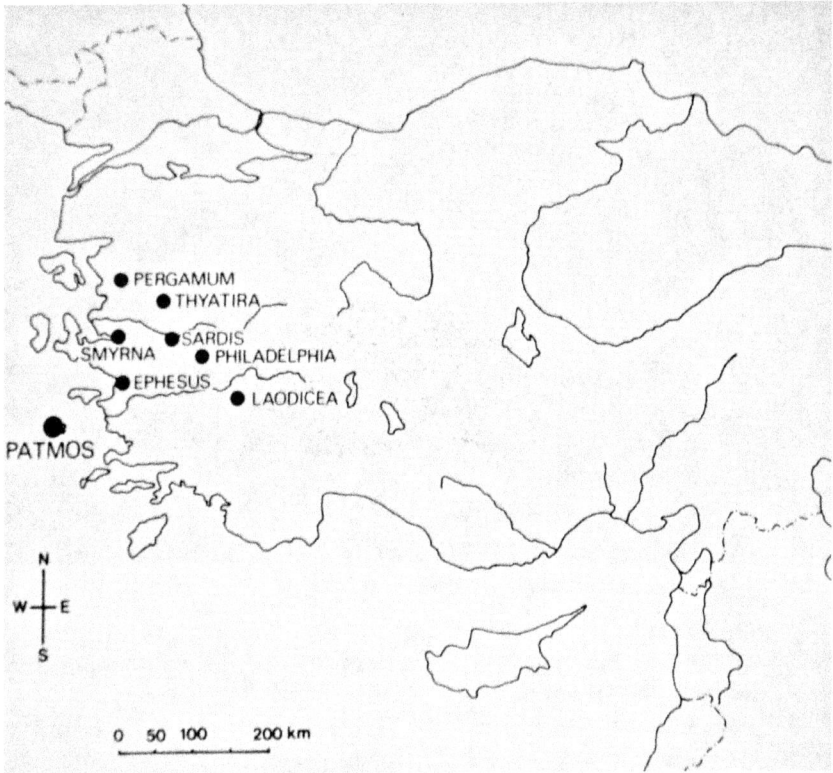

CHAPTER ONE

PATMOS

Surprises often come in tiny packets. Sometimes God uses that approach because we are unprogrammed for events in the Bethlehems and Nazareths of our world. We view them as ordinary, dull and bland and yet they are chosen of God as depots for his fantastic revelations.

For example, even the Apostle Paul was amazed at the philanthropy of a tiny, impoverished, Greek-cultured church in Macedonia. He hardly expected the welling up of generosity to come out of a congregation so young and so distant from God's people in Palestine, mostly of an alien Jewish culture. His surprise is recorded in his second letter to the church in Corinth: *"They did not do as we expected"* (2 Corinthians 8:5a).

Among God's surprises is the island of Patmos. It still possesses no airport. Unpretentious to say the least, it became a trader's trans-shipment centre, as well as prison and penal colony for thieves, exiled individuals, malcontents, citizens out-of-favour, Roman dissidents and troublemakers. Sailors trans-shipped their wares to and from Patmos' safe harbour. Roman emperors often chose Patmos as the terminus for their outcasts.

One is wistful upon entering the island's harbour. The protection of the hills calms the sometimes rumpled sea as one's water transport progressively nears the port town of Skala. The most obvious landmark of the island is its imposing fortress atop the island's highest hill (at the town Chora), overlooking the lovely, well-protected harbour. The monastery cannot be missed; it gives a visitor an impression that whatever else one sees on Patmos, the island honours the vision of Christ for his church. It dominates the island.

Patmos' Mythical Past

In the legends of myth, the Greek god Poseidon set his foot (*pato*) on the island. So, for a while the island was called Patmos. Before that it was named Letois. It had commercial connections with Miletus, a city of no mean stature on the southwest corner of Turkey (then Asia Minor).

Soon enough Rome possessed Patmos. And in mythology it served as a devotional temple site for Diana. Greek legends add the deity Selene (the moon goddess) who shed moonlight on the submerged island. She petitioned Diana. Diana drew the island above the water, assisted by her twin brother Apollo who, in turn, discussed this act with Zeus who permitted the creation. Zeus allowed the sun to dry off the island so that humans could inhabit the beautiful land. Let the reader untangle the knots of Greek legends!

When the book of *Revelation* was penned, some of these beliefs were still held by Patmos' inhabitants. It is not

22

impossible to see that the mysterious language of *Revelation* was partly understood by both Island and Mainland Greeks who held on to their religion system. Religion, fanciful as Greek mythology was, provided them with stability and with cohesion. Patmos' residents built a temple to Diana (Artemis) and to Apollo. The Apollo temple fell into disrepair with the advent of Christianity. A temple to Zeus also fell into disrepair and its site is no longer known. The temple to Diana (Artemis) was supplanted by the Orthodox monastery begun by Christodoulos in AD 1088.

Patmos' Political Overseers

Patmos was scarcely important to Rome, overseers of the island in biblical times. The adjacent islands were settled by Dorians and Ionians. Patmos had little by way of water supply, so it did not go begging for settlers. For a while, Patmos fell under the rule of Athens. Certainly Miletus shaped the economy of the island as a trans-shipping port. Rome took charge of Patmos in the second century BC.

A succession of raids by Normans, and Saracens left the island population in tatters but the monastery did not succumb to invaders. The next invasion was by the Crusaders, namely the Knights of St. John. There followed a rule by Turkish overseers who governed the island for almost 400 years except for a time of independence during a Russian/Turkish war.

When Greece's independence was acknowledged in the 1832 Treaty of Constantinople, Greece *almost* had possession of Patmos. Italy was Patmos' next occupier, followed by Germany. In 1948 Greece took possession of all the Dodecanese Islands in the Aegean, one of which is Patmos.

The island remains Greek. The Christodoulos Monastery is now the second largest training ground for seminarians of the Greek Orthodox Church.

Roman Barbarism

Is it true, as James L. Blevins suggests in his book, *Revelation As Drama*, that John was banished to Patmos because he criticized the adoration of Domitian worshiped in the form of a 16-foot statue of the emperor in the main square of Ephesus? Others surmise that John went there as a missionary.

Indeed, John may have moved from Ephesus to Patmos to share his faith with islanders and Roman militia. Along the waterfront of Skala, lie some ruins, protected by an iron grating. A sign claims that the ruin is from a basilica founded by John in AD 96. Certainly, the Orthodox monks believe this. However, John was not much interested in building basilicas, we suggest, but in sharing his faith with others. Who knows? These are interesting possibilities and theories.

If tradition is correct that John was a prisoner of Rome on Patmos, what was he doing there? Of the outcasts relegated to Patmos' quarries, none is better known than John. Is the writer of *Revelation* the same one who wrote the letters and the gospels? If so, he was a very old man when he was domiciled on Patmos. Variously called John the Disciple, John the Apostle, John the Theologian, John the Divine, this follower of Jesus of Nazareth joined the inelegant company who, with the Roman garrison, populated paltry Patmos.

That John was in Patmos should not have been entirely unpredictable. Strong traditions tell of John the Disciple moving to the Asia Minor area as a missionary of the cross. He is traced to Ephesus, a mere 100 kilometres' sail from Patmos, where a church named after him, a magnificent Byzantine Cathedral that doubled as a fortress, honoured his missionary work. Some tradition survived, although it is a most tenuous one, that the disciple brought the mother of Jesus to his home in Ephesus. Some Christians believe she died there in Ephesus.

It is generally believed that the gospel of John was written in the area of Ephesus and that it was the last of the gospels to be written. At least Irenaeus suggests that. Some scholars, i.e., John A. T. Robinson, argue that the entire New Testament was written by AD 70. Others believe that the gospel of John may have been later, even as late as AD 95. The timing of Revelation is generally believed to be during the Domitian period and its persecutions, possibly about AD 95. This writer nods to that suggestion.

No one knows indisputably. Nor does anyone know for certain that the author of John's gospel and that of *Revelation* are the same person. We happen to believe it is the same person. It could be true – but does it matter, really? It is God's word, after all, and John penned only what he was told to write.

Patmos' Location

Patmos is situated among the Dodecanese Islands of Greece. Geology suggests a different origin of these islands than the myth of Diana raising it from below the sea. These are volcanic islands, and Patmos is in the middle of them. Volcanic action pushed the island up from below and erosion smoothed off the rough places to where it is today, an island 13 miles (20 kms.) in one direction and 10 (16 kms) in another with a narrow neck of land separating the two highest points. Patmos is located about 30 miles (50 kilometers) from the Turkish coast. It was a great launching pad to send this mysterious letter to the "Seven Churches."

John spends little time discussing himself in the book of *Revelation*. The book is primarily, he says, about a vision he has been given by his Lord. It is a *revelation* (Latin) or *apocalupsis* (Greek) that suggests an uncovering, unveiling or removal of an obstacle to show things that had been hidden. John says that this vision and these words are those of Jesus Christ (1:2; 1:9).

His own part in this is to share the vision. As to why he was on this penal colony, we have only this information: "*I John, your brother and companion in the suffering and kingdom and patient endurance that are ours in Jesus was on the island of Patmos because of the word of God and the testimony of Jesus.*"

That possibly suggests he was a victim of the most recent persecutions that plagued the last decade of the 1st century. These were the orders of the Emperor Domitian who determined, that among other treasonous acts in the empire, was the decision of Christians to give unswerving allegiance to Jesus, the Christ and Lord. How could Christians honour both Jesus and Domitian as Lord? How indeed?

How much freedom John possessed in his apparent captivity is open for discussion. The apostle Paul enjoyed a remarkable freedom to preach and teach even while he was a prisoner in shackles during his Roman sojourn. Possibly John possessed such freedom. What he did not have was the freedom to write in the common language. Thus he employed the language of *apocalupsis*. This was a form of code, used by the book of Daniel to maintain community spirituality in the wake of secularism imposed by the tyrant Antiochus Epiphanes when the Temple was profaned a couple of centuries before the ministry of Jesus.

Blevins rightly describes these codes as three-fold. One is a colour code, each colour symbolic of a truth being revealed. A second code is that of numbers, for the numbers are symbolic, not literal. The third code is represented by animals, each one signifying a truth to be understood. When the codes are understood, *Revelation's* message comes through more clearly.

Of course there are other codes. Each is to be understood by particular geography and history associated with the area being addressed. We shall see these as we progress through the entire Circle of Seven churches. Whatever freedom John enjoyed in writing this final book of the Bible, it is evident that without the symbolic language of the coding, the letter to the churches would not have been carried in the postal section or by a private messenger on one of Domitian's galleys from the harbour of Patmos.

Patmos' Welcome Seclusion

A visit to Patmos is restorative for any modern pilgrim. The absence of an airport is a bonus. The climate is accommodating, with summer heat relieved by sea breezes. The communities offer relatively humble hostelries of assorted star value. Modest eateries offer simple menus at inexpensive costs. Walking is easy on the port walkways, and even in the hilltop villages – although getting there is a muscular challenge. Beaches on the warm Aegean waters are within walking range for the most part, or by caique to the remote places.

Best of all, soaking in the ambience of the monastery's chapels is an opportunity to reflect on God's plan for the ages. The various rooms of the hilltop monastery are replete with ancient frescoes, some dating back to the 12th century. The frescoes tell biblical stories or the activities (or deaths) of the sainted monks who dwelt there. Chants from the inner chambers of worshipping clerics provide a placid atmosphere for any traveller to reflect upon. The grotto, the "sacred" cave where Orthodox leaders claim John received the apocalyptic vision to write, is itself a powerful prayer room.

As we noted, tradition says that this monastery rests upon the former site of a temple to Artemis (Diana). Tradition adds that the founder of the monastery, Holy Christodoulos, broke the statue of Artemis from the temple into pieces and buried it under the foundations of the Byzantine monastery.

A visit to the monastery is an essential part of visiting Patmos. Guests are welcome to see the fortress and also its treasures collected from its earliest days. As soon as one visits the Greek Orthodox monastery he or she is reminded that this is a special place. The visitor is handed a brochure, which in polite terms, asks that the newcomer observe the respect that the monastery deserves. The brochure reads:

> Your coming to this island, the Ark of Christianity and unique treasury of history and legend, monuments and heirlooms, natural beauty and simple island life, is God's chosen gift to you.
>
> We welcome you with love. Our doors and our hearts are open to you. Your stay here shall be a 'school and cure for souls.' You shall worship [in] the Holy Cave wherein Saint John the Theologian wrote his Book of Revelation at the end of the 1st century AD.
>
> You shall visit the Great Monastery which the Hosios Christodoulos built at the chrysobulle command of Emperor Alexis Komnenos (sic) I in 1088.
>
> You shall see the fabulous wealth of holy heirlooms in the Treasury, all the valuable manuscripts and books of the Library, the countless churches, the old lordly buildings of the Middle Ages at Chora and the small white hospitable houses of the island.
>
> You shall enjoy the bright beaches and calm waters. You shall find voluntary and hearty hospitality everywhere in the island.
>
> Our only request is this: Respect the Holy Places, our traditions and our morals by your dignified attire, serious appearance and your general behaviour. In this way your stay here shall be fruitful, our acquaintance shall become real friendship and the memory of your visit shall reward your expectations and shall be worthy of the island's history. We shall really be very sorry if we shall be obliged to prohibit the entrance to our Holy Places of Worship to anyone not conforming to the above.

Thanking you, 'The Holy Monastery of Saint John the Theologian.'

The monastery may be reached by a very long climb by foot or an easy lift by bus. Upon each visit to Patmos this writer has climbed by foot, not because of a need for self-punishment but because the various vistas *en route* to the monastery change dramatically with each twist in the rising roadway. Moreover, partway to the top is the cave set aside as consecrated. In this cave, it is alleged by tradition, Saint John the Divine received his apocalypse and then dictated it to his supposed amanuensis, the disciple, scribe and deacon Prochorus (Acts 6:5). Perhaps it is better to take the bus to the top and walk down.

The entrance into the venerated grotto is unelaborate. Invariably, a soft drink and ice cream vendor stands on the pathway leading into the modest chapel complex. He knows that anyone walking up from the town or down from the monastery will find his wares attractive. Perhaps the visitor would like some post card of the monastery? Thirsty? He has a beverage to slake the need. Perhaps the visitor needs a new leather belt. It is here for you!

The outside walls of the inner building are white, as are so many Greek island residences. The objective is to reflect the light and not absorb it in the heat of a Grecian summer. Everywhere bougainvillaeas bloom with their variety of shades of aqua, garnet, scarlet, persimmon and lavender. The entry to the sacred cave provides a welcome and colourful introduction inside a place where wondrous things were revealed to a significant disciple of the Lord Jesus Christ.

Atop the cave are modest whitewashed buildings owned and operated by the Greek Orthodox community. Inside the cave are benches for worshippers who have come to pray and meditate in silence. Ahead of the benches is an iconostasis (the wall of icons) used in all Greek Orthodox Church buildings. This rather oriental tradition suggests that icons are windows through which realities of the kingdom are shown and made known.

The darkness of the cave is not complete but in its man-made twilight details of the images are very hard to observe. On the wall of the cave is a fresco that was discovered when whitewash began to peel in 1973. A depiction, several centuries old and in disrepair, shows John dictating to Prochorus. Over John's head are the letters *O A IO O THEOLOGOS*, representing the words, "The Holy John, The Divine." Divine used in this sense does not mean God, but "the one who interprets divine teaching." Another sign tells tourists that photographs are forbidden because of the holy nature of the sanctuary – no icons are allowed of the icons!

Entrance to the Byzantine monastery founded by the Holy Christodoulos is limited to special visiting hours. Appropriate – modesty, please! – clothing is required of visitors. If one is present at the opportune time one may observe and hear the monks being invited into The Chapel of the Holy Virgin to worship. This is marked in the intense rhythmic drumming by a monastery resident.

On the exterior wall of and vaulted entrance to the chapel is a host of frescoed icons depicting the biblical stories, with their strong emphasis on the miracles, and prophetic events which pointed to Jesus and his ministry, i.e., the story of Jonah and the great fish. Needless to say, strong in this motif is the emphasis upon Jesus' life, death, resurrection and consecration of apostles. These frescoes range in age from the more modern (!) ones of about 1745 back to the 12th century.

Visitors may enter the courtyard and chapel of the monastery without charge. But upstairs and in another room, for a token fee, one may visit the treasury. Here are displayed ancient manuscripts, vestments, furnishings used in the Eucharist and baptism, and other valuable museum pieces. Fragments from a 6th century manuscript of the gospel of Mark are in this monastery. Russian czars, such as Catherine II and Peter the Great, have given some of the jewels and icons. If one travels as far as the monastery, one should not deny oneself the privilege of viewing these consecrated objects.

The Greek Orthodox clergy virtually rule this tender island – but with a gentle hand. Their authority is vested in the bull from the emperor, Alexius I Comnenus (various spellings). He issued it from Constantinople in 1088. The "term" bull means edict or pronouncement. The term comes from the Latin word, *bulla*.

The terms of their dominion has been respected generally even during foreign occupations. Once again under Greek rule, this island has enjoyed the gentle but firm moral oversight of the monastery as its aforementioned brochure handout to visitors indicates.

One of the occupations in which a visitor may indulge while he or she visits this island of leisurely pace is to contemplate the activities of soldiers and sailors who once frequented the harbour of Skala. Over a Greek salad and Greek coffee in the patio of outdoor restaurants along the quays of Skala, one may consider how Roman patrols scoured the waterfront for signs of convicts intent on escaping the hard life of the quarries. Not to worry about drinking water! A desalination plant on the Island removes vestiges of salt and purifies the water.

Perhaps the visitor to the upper town of Chora will stroll its irregular lanes and look at door handles! Many of them take the shape of a hand, usually with a ring on the middle finger. Does this not say to the Patmos Islanders something which Jesus dictated to John for enscripting? *"I correct and discipline those whom I love, so be serious and repent! Look! I am standing at the door and knocking. If anyone listens to my voice and opens the door, I will come in to him and eat with him, and he will eat with me"* (3:19–20).

This writer has visited Greece many times and on several occasions stopped at Patmos – always by ship. We have travelled between Ikaria and Patmos, Piraeus and Patmos, Mikonos and Patmos, Rhodes, Kos and Patmos. But the most memorable was a journey we recall (thanks to an active imagination) between the Turkish coast to Samos and Patmos. Undoubtedly this is the route that was taken by the book of *Revelation*.

If one's imagination runs rampant he might envision the messenger and amanuensis Prochorus handing over for inspection his manuscript to Roman port workers who blue-pencilled both mail and messages. Undoubtedly the Roman authority censoring that document threw his hands in the air and muttered to himself, "Who can understand this?"

Readers who peruse *Revelation* without knowing that it is written in code are still asking that question raised by Roman censors. What follows in the next chapters will help us understand what Jesus Christ the Lord was saying to those who "had ears to hear," what the Spirit was saying to the churches. Many a reader has thrown up his hands, as did our supposed Roman censorship official. But those who are willing to learn the codes will find the key to the book.

The Uncoded Message from Patmos

Certainly not all of Revelation is in code. Here is an example (1:1–8):

> The revelation from Jesus Christ, which God gave him to show his servants what must soon take place. He made it known by sending his angel to his servant John, who testifies to everything he saw—that is, the word of God and the testimony of Jesus Christ. Blessed is the one who reads aloud the words of this prophecy, and blessed are those who hear it and take to heart what is written in it, because the time is near.
>
> John, To the seven churches in the province of Asia: Grace and peace to you from him who is, and who was, and who is to come, and from the seven spirits before his throne, and from Jesus Christ, who is the faithful witness, the firstborn from the dead, and the ruler of the kings of the earth.
>
> To him who loves us and has freed us from our sins by his blood, and has made us to be a kingdom and priests to serve his God and Father—to him be glory and power for ever and ever! Amen.
>
> "Look, he is coming with the clouds,"
>   and "every eye will see him,

even those who pierced him";
and all peoples on earth "will mourn because of him."
So shall it be! Amen. "I am the Alpha and the Omega,"
*   says the Lord God, "who is, and who was, and who*
*   is to come, the Almighty."*

This part is relatively uncoded because John wants to make perfectly clear who is the author of the vision to follow, what authority John has for penning the contents of the letters, who are the recipients and what are the blessings from reading, accepting and obeying it. "Seven spirits" means the fullness and complete presence of the Holy Spirit.

The events given in the vision will soon unfold. The words are to be read aloud, so that all recipients will hear audibly what the written word is all about. God's word will be a blessing to those who take it to heart. Jesus is coming!

First, John states the reality of the exalted Jesus. Pay heed, he is no ordinary man! Jesus is the "resurrected" man! He is the ruler over every earthly kingdom and earthly emperor. He loved us. He liberated us from our sins. He honoured us by including us in his kingdom (as opposed to the way the Roman kingdom works). He privileged us by ordaining us to his priesthood. Jesus has named us as servants of God the Father.

Next, John tells of his Lord's glorious return, not in secret but in full view of all humanity. Even those who put him to death, or persist in destroying him in one way or another will view his epiphany and rue the days they railed against him.

Then John identifies the exalted Jesus as *Alpha* and *Omega* (first and last letters of the Greek alphabet, *aleph* and *tav* in the Hebrew alphabet). He is eternal – was, is and shall be. He authored creation. He will preside over the end of history. He will rule in between. Jesus' sovereignty is all inclusive. Let no reader miss the point.

The Patmos Vision

Note that the message (1:9–18) that follows is (a) local, (b) an admonition to all churches everywhere in all time, (c) personal (if you have an ear, listen up!) and (d) prophetic.

> *I, John, your brother and companion in the suffering and kingdom and patient endurance that are ours in Jesus, was on the island of Patmos because of the word of God and the testimony of Jesus. On the Lord's Day I was in the Spirit, and I heard behind me a loud voice like a trumpet, which said: "Write on a scroll what you see and send it to the seven churches: to Ephesus, Smyrna, Pergamum, Thyatira, Sardis, Philadelphia and Laodicea."*
>
> *I turned around to see the voice that was speaking to me. And when I turned I saw seven golden lampstands, and among the lampstands was someone like a son of man, dressed in a robe reaching down to his feet and with a golden sash around his chest. The hair on his head was white like wool, as white as snow, and his eyes were like blazing fire. His feet were like bronze glowing in a furnace, and his voice was like the sound of rushing waters. In his right hand he held seven stars, and coming out of his mouth was a sharp, double-edged sword. His face was like the sun shining in all its brilliance.*

When I saw him, I fell at his feet as though dead.
Then he placed his right hand on me and said: "Do
not be afraid. I am the First and the Last. I am the
Living One; I was dead, and now look, I am alive for
ever and ever! And I hold the keys of death and
Hades.

Initially, John identifies himself as one among his
fellow sufferers. In this section we read of depictions, not
coded, but descriptive of a person having majestic worth and
honour. It is Jesus himself. He is among the privileged of
God whose endurance is being tested. He is a companion in
suffering along with those elsewhere mentioned in this
writing. He writes from the experience of suffering. He
knows what severe hardships his faith-family is enduring for
the sake of Jesus and his kingdom.

John then explains the instruction to write this
apocalyptic letter. The vision occurred on "the Lord's Day,"
i.e. the day of Jesus' resurrection. These seven church letters
all rolled into one letter, come at the command of Christ
himself. Christ also is among the suffering churches. He
stands among the *menorah* lampstands (the churches giving
light to the world) even as he dictates his holy word to John.
Jesus' voice is authoritative. He sounds like the trumpet
calling troops to a battle – loud and clear. His voice is
unmuffled just as the message is authentic and distinctive.

Other descriptive words highlight the greatness of
Jesus. He is white-haired, a signal of his authority. His
distinctive judgmental robe is white. His piercing eyes blaze
like a fire. His feet resemble a blacksmith's furnace.

He wields a Roman-type two-edged sword meting out justice and signalling his victory. *"The sword of the Spirit is God's word,"* as Paul told Ephesian believers (6:17), In Hebrews (4:12), we note that the word of God (i.e., the gospel) is *"living and active, and sharper that any double-edged sword, penetrating even to dividing soul and spirit, joints and marrow; it judges the thoughts and attitudes of the heart."* With his sword, Jesus will conquer and win victory. Jesus' face is like the sun itself, almost too brilliant to look into as it meets the morning.

John is so overcome by the sight that he falls in shock, reverence and awe before the Lord of life and history. But the exalted Jesus places his sword hand on John with a touch of assurance. He has dropped the sword in so affirming John. The Lord bids him to fear not. His is the power, his the authority. His is the creation and the terminus of human history! He lived and died and still lives because he conquered sin and death. He will live eternally and he holds the keys to provide eternal life and eternal death.

Jesus' Order to Write

John makes clear once more that neither is he the author of what follows, nor is the motivation for writing his own decision. His writing is in obedience to the First and the Last. The implication is that anyone receiving the letter must also be in subjugation to Jesus' will. He lives and imparts life to anyone.

We see John's hesitancy as he listens to his Lord. In the presence of One so exalted, does not everyone reflect on his own unworthiness to be a channel of God's message?

Yet, when one realizes that God sanctifies us to do his work we can rejoice in the trust he has placed in weak disciples – *"clay fragile pots"* (2 Corinthians 4:7). In the same chapter, Paul assures believers we need not fear our glorified Saviour. *"We who with unveiled faces all reflect the Lord's glory are being transformed into his likeness with ever-increasing glory which comes from the Lord, who is the Spirit."*

So John continued to record what Jesus was saying to him and to all believers locally, everywhere and for all time.

Therefore, write down what you have seen, what is, and what is going to happen after this. The secret meaning of the seven stars that you saw in my right hand and the seven gold lampstands is this: the seven stars are the messengers of the seven churches, and the seven lampstands are the seven churches (1:19, 20).

Stars are messengers. They direct traffic, especially ships at sea in the blackest part of the night. The churches mentioned must understand that its members are always being observed. Moreover, they will continue to be blessed by God's messages. All God's precious churches will always have a means of communication with God himself. John sees the full Church, completed, diverse, yet united, and entire as it gathers at the end of time before the presence of Jesus in all his glory.

Messengers are pastors. Alternatively, and more likely, stars represent the pastors of the church. Imagine! Pastors have star power in this book. Pastors are guiding lights given to the church by God himself.

It was Christ who gave some to be apostles, some to be prophets, some to be evangelists and some to be pastors and teachers, to prepare God's people for works of service so that the body of Christ may be built up in unity in the faith and in the knowledge of the Son of God and become mature, attaining to the whole measure of the fullness of Christ (Ephesians 4:11 *ff*).

In summary, we can say the keys of "life and death" which Jesus holds will tell us that when Jesus Christ is fully revealed, all of creation will honour, praise and adore him in his worthiness. Know that God controls everything. His rule is all-inclusive. When that happens, then Rome, Babylon, the number of the beast or whatever code name you use for human power will be seen for what it is, bankrupt and inconsequential.

CHAPTER TWO

EPHESUS

To the angel of the church in Ephesus write:
These are the words of him who holds the seven stars
in his right hand and walks among the seven golden
lampstands: I know your deeds, your hard work and
your perseverance. I know that you cannot tolerate
wicked men, that you have tested those who claim to
be apostles but are not, and have found them false.
You have persevered and have endured hardships for
my name, and have not grown weary.
Yet I hold this against you: You have forsaken your
first love. Remember the height from which you have
fallen! Repent and do the things you did at first. If
you do not repent, I will come to you and remove
your lampstand from its place. But you have this in
your favor: You hate the practices of the Nicolaitans,

which I also hate.
He who has an ear, let him hear what the Spirit says
to the churches. To him who overcomes, I will give
the right to eat from the tree of life, which is in the
paradise of God (Revelation 2:1–7).

As the caique set its course from Patmos harbour, past Samos to Ephesus, Prochorus undoubtedly reflected on the symbols used in the holy correspondence entrusted to his care. Ephesus was an old city even in the time of John. The city was founded about the time King David acceded to Samuel's call to be anointed in preparation for his becoming King of Israel and Judah. The area around Ephesus was inhabited as many as 8,000 years before Christ.

Even a Greek who had been won into the kingdom of God from his pagan origins must have understood in the roots of his new faith, the mystery of the *menorah*. It was the sacred candle light representing God in Jerusalem's now-destroyed Jerusalem Temple, and before that in the Tabernacle. In Jesus' time it had nine branches. That was because two branches had been added at the time of the Jewish exile. "Seven" was a more suitable number than nine. In effect, when the Lord talked about seven candles giving light, he was urging the letter's recipients to return to basics. Nine was an add-on; seven was the original. Seven was complete.

Seven, as we cannot emphasize enough, was a perfect number to the Hebrew people. Creation was summed up in seven days. The number of God was 777. As we noted in the introduction, when Peter asked Jesus if he should forgive someone seven times, that was a symbolic statement. It represented perfect forgiveness. Jesus responded with an answer that was even more symbolic. "Seventy-seven times," said the Lord. That represented "perfect plus" forgiveness.

So there are "seven churches" mentioned in the book of Revelation. By no means were they the only churches in the area. In fact, the idea of seven churches really means that the word from God was intended for every church and for all the churches.

Note that the sense of "all" is further indicated in the linking of the churches in their order. Take a map, join the jots, and very quickly it is apparent that the Seven Churches of Asia Minor were in a rough circle. They were a "Circle of Seven."

Note that each church is addressed in seven sections. First is the identification of the church being addressed. Next is a reference to attributes of Christ. Third we see a description of the spiritual audit of that church. Following that is an exhortation with regard to the audit. Sixth is a promise to those who heed the warning. Seventh and last is a call to listen to God's Spirit tell the truth about his church.

Other numbers are similarly important. If seven is a "perfect," six is "imperfect." Two means support or companionship, which is symbolized in the commission of Jesus to his disciples to go out "two-by-two," and to the animals in Noah's Ark who came in two-by-two. Three also represented a divine number but three-and-a-half is a number representing imperfection and chaos. Four as a number meant the visible creation, and when added to the divine number three, became seven, the complete number. Ten was used as human completeness. Twelve signified organized religious life, i.e., the twelve tribes, the twelve disciples.

These numbers, together with their multiples, help to unlock the code.

Even the figures described in the book were written in symbolic form. John manages to name Jesus in the text. For the most part, however it was dangerous to speak of Christ in a setting where affirming Christ resulted in execution. Most of the time John uses symbols to speak of Christ. So the figure of Daniel 7:13 is employed and combines the term "Ancient of Days" together with "Son of Man." "Angels" also meant "messengers." The word used for "church" (*ekklesia*) also meant town council. Roman censors had neither time, patience nor insight to come to grips with such double entendre terminology.

One cannot neglect some other symbols in the book. The words kingdom, tribulation and patient endurance have more than one meaning. They refer in part to the current persecution by the emperor and suggest that the hurtfulness will get worse. However, the equation has another part to it. This was sent to people living in an area where the heresy of Gnosticism was rampant. Gnostics denied that Christ was incarnate. Some of them argued that Jesus was a man but a divine nature descended upon him for a while, arriving at his baptism, departing before his crucifixion. *Revelation*, like John's gospel, John's letters and Paul's letter to Colossians, fights Gnosticism.

Perhaps that is one reason for Jesus' use of a "sharp two edged sword" (Revelation 1:16). There were two enemies to the church, (1) persecution without and (2) heresy within. The two-edged sword cut two ways, for God's word is both the means of salvation to those who receive it and a judgment upon those who do not. Better to be true to one's faith and correct in one's belief than to accept the judgment of an emperor or heretics over that of God.

Time has done an injustice to Ephesus. The wonderful harbour that once welcomed and farewelled ships from every corner of the empire, like that of Miletus, is now so silted up that the sea is miles away. The Cayster River (Caystros was the river deity), on which it was founded, has simply carried eroded soil downstream, seaward. Soil has filled what was the former dockside section of the city.

It is harder, therefore, for us to imagine the emotional responses of people on that caique on which Prochorus had embarked, as they approached the broad harbour of that majestic city. Chances are, they gasped at its dignity. From far out in the Aegean, the impressive temple of Artemis would have been visible to maritime travellers. It was, after all, one of the wonders of the ancient world, with fantastic friezes and its great statue of the divine Artemis as the focus of its magnificent layout. The residents of Ephesus in Paul's time, attributed the city's founding to the earth goddess Artemis (the Roman Diana, the Phrygian Cybele) but the historian Herodotos proposed that the city's mythological founder was Ephos, queen of the Amazons. Is this where Ephesus gets its name?

The Greek goddess Artemis and the great Phrygian goddess Cybele were identified together as *Artemis of Ephesus*. The many-breasted deity of Ephesus, identified with Artemis, was venerated in the Temple of Artemis, one of the Seven Wonders of the World. It was the largest building of the ancient world according to Pausanias who mentions that the temple was built by Ephesus, son of the river god Caystrus before the immigration of the Ionians. Scarcely a trace remains of this structure.

There is little left of this temple which once was announced as a wonder of the world. Parts of a pillar stand tenuously from its base, but its segments could easily topple in a medium-sized earthquake. The temple to Artemis was approximately four times larger than Athens' Parthenon, and every piece as beautiful in form. Its platform was 126.5 meters in length by 73 meters in width. The actual temple's dimensions were slightly less than that but its 117 pillars of almost 17 meters in height reportedly were made from a single stone and were individually sculpted. The remaining pillar still standing certainly is not made from one piece of stone.

This temple went through several "incarnations." The version referred to in scripture was ordered constructed by Alexander the Great. He had learned it had been destroyed on the day he was born. When it was rebuilt, it lasted for some 500 years. The Artemision, as the temple was dubbed, honoured Artemis (Diana), a pagan deity referred to in the biblical book of *Acts*. *Acts* details Paul's three year ministry in Ephesus. *"Men of Ephesus, doesn't all the world know that the city of Ephesus is the guardian of the temple of the great Artemis and of her image which fell from heaven?"*

Paul was dancing on eggs while residing for three years at Ephesus. When some idol makers converted from paganism to follow Jesus they gave up their lucrative employment of providing miniature silver replicas of Artemis (Acts 19:23 *ff.*). Other silversmiths saw this decline in sales as an economic threat and couched their concerns wrapping them in an insult against their local deity. Paul's missionary ministry was about to suffer. One must always take care to not demean any local traditions, not that Paul had. An amphitheatre holding 24,000 protesters is a formidable opposition. Fortunately, saner heads prevailed. Paul was spirited out of town by his friends. The complaints were turned over to a court to resolve. Paul reluctantly agreed to let local Christians deal with the issue.

Artemis was also known in Roman mythology as Diana. The idol was famous for its many breasts. The breasts may not have been breasts at all but testicles of bulls. No matter – the image is one of fertility and prosperity. A copy of this idol is in the museum at Ephesus and another version is to be found in Rome's Vatican Museum. Worship of this goddess was understood to be the reason for the great success of Ephesus as a world city. Indeed, world city that it was, it boasted a population in John's time similar to that of Corinth. It was the main city of the province of Asia.

What would be interesting is to know how the mean-spirited emperor, Titus Flavius Domitian, could have tolerated any devotion to Artemis when he refused any compromise for Christians. Christians, in the face of a death sentence, boldly stated, *christos kurios* "Jesus is Lord!" instead of *kaisar kurios*, "Caesar is Lord!"

The Roman despot Domitian ordained that a temple built to him should also be erected in Ephesus. He also demanded that public worship be offered to him as *Dominus et Deus*, "Lord and God." He must have been wily enough to recognize that any disturbance of the worship activities in the Artemision would have amounted to a total city revolt against his authority.

Visible from an even further distance at sea would have been the city's astonishing Great Theatre. In Paul's time, when he was the subject of a massing of Ephesian citizens, the theatre was well on its way to completion. The reconstructed theatre that we can see today holds some 24,000 or more attenders.

A visitor strolling through the theatre might let his imagination go to work there. He should be able to let his mind's ear hear the clamour and shouts of irate Ephesians chanting, "Great is Artemis of the Ephesians." He might, in his mind's eye, see the unruly crowd seize Paul's travelling companions, Gaius and Aristarchus, who undoubtedly at that moment feared for their lives. And as they were seized we might imagine Paul being hustled by his friends onto an awaiting boat heading out of the harbour.

A generation and-a-half later, by the time John sent the Lord's correspondence to his church in Ephesus, the Great Theatre had many more additions, not just in its dimensions but in its stage amenities.

The city brothel was adjacent to the theatre's south wing, near the public baths. Perhaps this institution held some religious significance, just as in Corinth's infamous Temple of Aphrodite atop the Acrocorinth. More likely, this was the stopping place for merchants and sailors, gladiators (the winners, that is) and the general population. Asian society held few moral qualms about prostitution. The brothel's advertising sign was a footprint and a crown carved in the pavement.

It is significant for the tourist today, to see markers bearing images of gladiators placed directly opposite the city brothel on Marble Road, the street which links Curetes Street and the colonnaded Arcadia (Harbour) Street. As one sees these images, one remembers the words of Saint Paul to the Ephesians in chapter 6: *"Put on the whole armour of God so that you can take your stand against the devil's schemes . . ."*

Much of the grand reconstruction of Ephesus that each tourist will observe was constructed later than the New Testament period. Nonetheless, from the variety of temples built there, it is plain to see that like the Athenians, the Ephesians were a "very religious people." Temples abounded to gratify their many gods and goddesses. In addition, the buildings that honoured Trajan and Hadrian reflect the degree to which emperor worship gradually increased and took root.

Tourists visiting Ephesus today will get an eye-opening experience because the reconstruction is so widespread. One might harbour a temptation to think that this was the same Ephesus in which Paul spent three years of ministry and Saint John knew as a teacher of Christian doctrine. But it is not. Visitors today see a composite Ephesus, one spanning several centuries. At one end of the scale are the ruins of the Artemision. But ruins of church buildings constructed from the fifth century onward are also to be inspected.

One of these is the double church of St. Mary, so described because it has altars at both ends of the building. It is in the area near the harbour and main gymnasium of Ephesus. (A church with a Christian education wing?) A baptismal tank is set in the midst of the building's floor, indicating that immersion was in vogue during the early 5th century. It was a very large building, converted from pagan usage and remade into a basilica. In AD 431 it hosted the third ecumenical council of the church.

That council meeting was a significant one in defining – and dividing – Christian thought. The theme of the council was the place and work of Mary as the mother of Jesus. Names like Cyril and Nestorius were linked in the discussion. The term adopted by the Council was *Theotokos*, the "Mother of God." Cyril was patriarch of Alexandria and Nestorius, patriarch of Constantinople. They took opposite sides, or seemingly so, about the nature of Christ. Cyril received plaudits from the church and was referred to as *Pillar of Faith* and *Seal of all the Fathers*. Nestorius' views were rejected.

On the other hand, Nestorians called Cyril a heretic and destroyer of the church. Nestorius' doctrine emphasized a disunion between the human and divine natures of Jesus. Nestorius also rejected the title *Theotokos* (Mother of God) for the Virgin Mary. Nestorius and his teachings were also condemned as heretical at the Council of Chalcedon in 451. This resulted in the "Nestorian Schism" in which churches supporting Nestorius broke with the rest of the Church. The Christian Church of the East, located in Persia, became increasingly doctrinally Nestorian and sometimes was dubbed the Nestorian Church.

Another building of significance in Ephesus, or perhaps more accurately, just outside the city, was the Basilica of Saint John the Divine. More than one church structure graced this site, overlooking the ruins of the Artemision. The final church structure (the ruins are now visible to tourists) was ordered by the emperor Justinian in the latter half of the 6th century. It was a model of Byzantine architecture and was used later as a fortress when Arabs constantly besieged Ephesus over the following two centuries. The basilica boasts being the last earthly resting place of the author of *Revelation*.

The Ephesian Report Card

The Christian community in Ephesus was faced with a tremendous challenge to keep the faith and not to compromise its doctrines. That the people remained orthodox is given credence by the letter that Prochorus first took to the church in Ephesus. It tells us that the Christians worked hard, did "good," and persevered. The church obeyed the Johannine tenant that, *"Jesus performed many other signs in the presence of his disciples that are not recorded in this book. But these have been recorded so that you may believe that Jesus is the Christ, the Son of God, and so that through believing you may have life in his name"* John 20:30, 31).

These saints would let none of the doctrines held by pagans adulterate their Christ-centred beliefs. Moreover, in spite of the severe testing which was put to them, in spite of the compromises they were asked to accept in the name of faith, they maintained a vigorous set of beliefs that could never be challenged as heresy.

The letter of *Revelation* commends the church members for all this. It congratulates them for not allowing a heretical group known as the Nicolaitans from infiltrating their circle of faith and belief. Some early Church Fathers, such as Ignatius and Irenaeus, suggest that to be a Nicolaitan was to live promiscuously in order to celebrate their salvation.

Their theological rationalization appears to be that discussed by Saint Paul in his letter to the Romans (Romans 6:1), *"What shall we say then? Shall we go on sinning that grace may increase?"* The followers of Nicolas, if that is the origin of the "ism" he venerates, are similar to the Balaamites referred to in the letter (third in the sequence of seven) to Pergamum (*Revelation* 2:14). These followers of Nicolas were unrestrained in their sexual licence. That Ephesus rejected such beliefs and actions was noted by Jesus. He congratulated them for their sexual faithfulness and chaste behaviour amid such prominent debauchery.

So what's the challenge in this church at Ephesus? It's a problem of "going through the legal motions and maintaining the legalities." Legalism was the downfall of many legalists in Jesus' ministry. They saw salvation stemming from "doing," rather than from grace. Their faith resided in an era of legalism rather than in love. This church "did" a lot of things correctly but it lacked love in the doing of them. Saint Paul described love as greater than faith or hope (1 Corinthians 13). Legalism can be the enemy of love. The Church at Ephesus was pure but it did not love people the way the Saviour loved them. The trumpet call to Christians in Ephesus was to beckon them to be as loving in their relationships as they were true to their doctrines.

No doubt this charge by Jesus offended John as well. He knew well that Jesus gave a new commandment to love others even to the extent and in the way that Jesus loved everyone. *"I am giving you a new commandment to love one another,"* said Jesus. *"Just as I have loved you, you also should love one another. This is how everyone will know that you are my disciples, if you have love for one another"* (John 13:34, 35).

The impact of love as crucial to Christian behaviour is found in several places in John's letters. They obeyed John's injunction to not love worldly things. John wrote (1 John 1:5–7):

Stop loving the world and the things that are in the world. If anyone persists in loving the world, the Father's love is not in him. For everything that is in the world—the desire for fleshly gratification, the desire for possessions, and worldly arrogance—is not from the Father but is from the world. And the world and its desires are fading away, but the person who does God's will abides forever.

The Ephesian Christians must not have read the remainder of the epistle.

This is how we have come to know love: Christ gave his life for us. We, too, ought to give our lives for our brothers. Whoever has earthly possessions and notices a brother in need and yet withholds his compassion from him, how can the love of God abide in him? Little children, we must stop loving in word and in tongue, but instead love in action and in truth.
This is how we will know that we belong to the truth and how we will be able to establish our hearts in his presence. If our hearts condemn us, God is greater than our hearts and knows everything. Dear friends, if our hearts do not condemn us, we have confidence in the presence of God. Whatever we request we receive from him, because we keep his commandments and do what pleases him. And this is his commandment: to believe in the name of his Son, Jesus Christ, and to love one another as he commanded us. The person who keeps his commandments abides in God, and God abides in him. This is how we can be sure that he abides in us: he has given us his Spirit" (1 John 3:16–24).

Did not Jesus warn his disciples about legalism without love? This failure of faith is rooted in legalism and unrooted in love. *"How terrible it will be for you Pharisees! For you give a tenth of your mint, spices, and every kind of herb, but you neglect justice and the love of God. These are the things you should have practised, without neglecting the others. How terrible it will be for you Pharisees! For you love to have the places of honour in the synagogues and to be greeted in the marketplaces"* (Luke 11:42–43).

The Lord of the Ephesian Church has judged his people. Yet he gives them another chance to redeem things, He offers the church that reverses course an opportunity to inherit access to the new Garden of Eden. They may be eligible to partake of all the fruit once forbidden by God for samplers but now purified for nutrition of the saints. "You are warned," says Christ of his Church.

CHAPTER THREE
SMYRNA

*"To the angel of the church in Smyrna write:
These are the words of him who is the First and the
Last, who died and came to life again. I know your
afflictions and your poverty—yet you are rich! I
know about the slander of those who say they are
Jews and are not, but are a synagogue of Satan. Do
not be afraid of what you are about to suffer. I tell
you, the devil will put some of you in prison to test
you, and you will suffer persecution for ten days. Be
faithful, even to the point of death, and I will give
you life as your victor's crown.
Whoever has ears, let them hear what the Spirit says
to the churches. Those who are victorious will not be
hurt at all by the second death"* (Revelation 2:8–11).

It's a guess as to how the book of *Revelation* was
ferried from Ephesus to the other churches mentioned as its
recipients. So let's guess. Suppose the scroll / letter moved
with Prochorus in a clockwise fashion to each of the
destinations. As we suggested, look at them on a map and
they become something of a circle of seven.

When he had left the first of the seven scrolls in Ephesus, Prochoros caught a ship heading northwards some 65 kilometers to the next main port in Asia Minor, namely Smyrna, dubbed the "Pearl of the Orient." As his transport entered the harbour of Smyrna, the bright sunlight gleaming on the soldiers' armour in the fortress on top of Mount Pagos, mirrored all the way to the quay where he docked.

"So this is the famous crown," thought Prochoros, remembering that Alexander the Great had ordered a fortification to be built upon the great hill overlooking Smyrna. Perhaps he knew it by the local moniker, "The Velvet Castle." This is unlikely, since the sobriquet is more modern. It was his "gift" to the city. "Gift" was Alexander's euphemism for his need to keep the subjects of Smyrna under the watchcare of his militia. Alexander's troops could cast a watchful eye on the streets below the "crown" to see if groups were massing unnaturally. They could also scan the coastline to see if an armada of enemy ships was massing for an invasion.

Undoubtedly, Prochoros also connected the "crown" given by Alexander to keep the people of Smyrna under his subjugation to the "crown" referred to in the letter he was carrying. By contrast, the crown that Jesus would give to the faithful of Smyrna's church was a crown of freedom and life.

Smyrna was a recognized city long before Alexander. In Homer's time it was well known. It is said that Homer was born in Smyrna. Some claim that Homer is buried in this city (Some also claim he was buried on the Greek island of Ios). There was even a temple to Homer and a theatre to Homer (The Homerion) in the city.

In its earliest period Smyrna was located a short distance across the bay from its biblical site. Alexander the Great was responsible for its move. Smyrna's name derived from the goddess Myrina, worshipped by the original Aeolian settlers. Alexander claimed that in a dream – so the story goes – the goddess Nemesis revealed to him a vision that the city should be moved approximately to where its ruins are found today from across the bay where Aeolians first settled. The cult of Nemesis was anchored to the city of Smyrna. A temple to her adoration was also found in Marathon. She was the divine spirit of retribution; a name for one's self being one's worst enemy. In the Greek mind she personified vengeful fate.

When Alexander died, Smyrna fell under the authority of Pergamum. Pergamum was a rising star in the territory of Lydia. An earthquake severely damaged the city of Smyrna in AD 178. Is this a connection with Nemesis here? Earthquakes have been a common occurrence in the general area.

When (and *if*) Prochorus visited Smyrna, he came to a metropolis, a large city, and a rival of Ephesus. It was replete with a mixture of oriental and Greek traditions. Smyrna was known as the "Pearl of the Orient" because of its lovely setting and grand avenues, one of which was called Golden Street. Today, the Turkish city of Izmir, which rises on the foundations of Smyrna, is similarly set in a scintillating panorama along the shores of the Aegean.

There was also another application of "crown" connected to this city. Its main deity was Cybele whose image on coinage was always that of a queen, crown to match. Cybele was the chief deity of Smyrna and was referred to by her priests as "the glory of Asia." Cybele was not much different in character and function than Artemis of the Ephesians.

Cybele is described as "the mother of the gods of Olympus." When her reference was translated from Greek into Roman mythology she was known as the *Magna Deum Mater*. The *Magna Mater* cult was one which had many strange behavioural aspects, including the drinking of bull's blood. As with most of the pagan gods, the element of fertility and success was behind the motivation of worship to Cybele and devotees expected such response.

Temples to many other mythological deities matched the multiple temples to Cybele. Zeus was honoured here. Aesklepios (various spellings), the god associated with healing, was a significant cult, and in fact, its priests were the physicians of the ancient world. Aphrodite, another of the fertility goddesses was venerated in Smyrna's temples by Smyrna's pagan worshippers. Cybele's worship often called for cultic prostitution in her temples. Apollo was also worshipped in Smyrna.

Later, as emperors increased their roles from governors to deities, the imperial cult erected temples to the Caesars. At one point, Smyrna's citizenry petitioned the Roman government to allow them to build a temple honouring Tiberius as both emperor and god. This action had precedence for this; almost 300 years prior to the writing of *Revelation*, a temple to Dea Roma was the first in the world to be built – right in Smyrna.

There was at least one other important religion practised in Smyrna. Judaism was there. These Jewish citizens had fled their homeland during various dispersions. One traced from the time of the Babylonian captivity in 586 BC. Another diaspora was the result of the persecutions of the infamous Antiochus Epiphanes, some 135 years before Jesus was born. It was Antiochus who polluted the Jerusalem Temple by offering swine's flesh on the great altar. Yet one more wave of refugees spread across Asia Minor following the destruction of Jerusalem from AD 66 – 70.

The Jews had scattered in the various prosecutions. They fanned out from Jerusalem to many points in the Roman Empire and settled both comfortably and profitably in the cities mentioned in *Revelation*. Surprisingly, Jews were able to practise their faith without too much hindrance from the emperor, even though they would not acknowledge the emperor as being divine. They chose occupations that would not compromise their Sabbath observance, or dietary distinctions. Most managed to maintain kosher kitchens.

Employment that helped them celebrate their spiritual distinctives were not many. Most jobs called for ablutions to deities and most ablutions invited behaviour, such as orgies, which could seldom be modified sufficiently to allow Jews their ritual purity. The textile industry seemed to draw them in particular. So did banking! If Jews predominated in an industry then they would be less likely and less necessary to compromise their traditions and deportment to match the pagan expectations.

Jewish Persecution of Christians

The Christian presence in Smyrna appears to have been more of a problem to the Jewish community of that city than was its idolatry and emperor worship. In the era immediately following the persecutions connected with Caesar Domitian, the Jews joined the general persecution against the Christians. The Church Fathers, Justin Martyr and Tertullian, give evidence to that reality. Presiding over the trial of Polycarp (AD 156), the bishop and leader of the church, the proconsul Statius Quadratus found allies in Smyrna's Jewish community.

Polycarp was brought into the arena on a Sabbath, according to Irenaeus, where Jews joined the pagans in demanding his death. "This fellow is the teacher of Asia, the father of Christians, the destroyer of our gods, who teaches people not to sacrifice or worship." * (copyright 1950, Harper and Brothers, *The Apostolic Fathers*, E. J. Goodspeed pp. 250 - 252). Evidently, these Jews at once broke the Sabbath, entered a profane place and took part in a pagan execution. They gathered wood for the pyre. At each instance of this action, they would have broken their ritual purity and have transgressed the Decalogue. It was a case of "the enemy of my enemy is my friend."

When Polycarp was burned in the arena, his witness became a standard by which the Christians near and far took note. Messages were sent to various church communities with details of his trial brought on by the charges. So it was noted that Polycarp did not elect to escape his enemies even though it was conveniently arranged for him to do so. He rather voluntarily accepted arrest, entered the arena and politely refused yet another escape opportunity given to him to sacrifice to the emperor. He was told by Statius Quadratus to "swear by the fortune of Caesar and revile Christ." But the 86 year-old bishop (pastor) would not.

"For 86 years I have been his slave," said Polycarp, "and he has done me no wrong; how can I blaspheme my King who has saved me?" With that refusal he was judged guilty of treason and burned to death. But that persecution followed decades after the book of *Revelation* was penned. The book of *Revelation* simply points forward to what would take place among followers of Jesus who called him Lord and King.

When we turn to the book of *Revelation* we deduce much about the state of that Christian community in Smyrna when John sent the letter. Once again the letter is sent by way of a messenger (angel) that probably means the pastor who oversees the Church in Smyrna. This congregation had undergone a distress of some sort. The word *tribulation* is used to describe it. Additionally, the people in the congregation were destitute. The word (*ptocheia*) describing their poverty conveys the sense of unemployment. Perhaps they were unable to get work because of some boycotting in the market place, or from general persecution.

Likely, these Christians turned up on the sales stalls of the local market with a full crop to sell, but buyers purposely passed by, ignoring them. The sellers simply took their produce home with them. Eventually it went bad because there were no buyers.

These believers were slandered (*blasphemia*), according to the record in *Revelation*. Blasphemy, our English word from which the term "slander" derives, means abusing someone's reputation. When God's name was taken in vain, or misused, then this was blasphemy (Exodus 20:7; Acts 19:37).

61

The sense of the scripture is that the Jews, not the Roman officials, were responsible for this specific persecution. The term "synagogue of Satan" is used here as it refers to the experience of Jesus when a collection of Pharisees tried to repudiate Jesus for his discussion of true descendants of Abraham. Jesus said, *"Your father Abraham rejoiced that he would see my day, and he saw it and was glad." Then the Jews said to him, "You are not even fifty years old, yet you have seen Abraham?" Jesus said to them, "Truly, truly I tell you, before there was an Abraham, I am!" At this, they picked up stones to throw at him, but Jesus hid himself and went out of the Temple"* (John 8:56–59).

This group of legalists was too ready to condemn and too unprepared to love "unworthy" people (John 8:56 – 59). Sometimes condemning someone is based on personal threats to one's opinion because one has an insecure faith. To wit . . .

> *At daybreak he appeared again in the Temple, and all the people came to him. So he sat down and began to teach them. But the scribes and the Pharisees brought a woman who had been caught in adultery. After setting her before them, they said to him, "Teacher, this woman has been caught in the very act of adultery. Now in the Law, Moses commanded us to stone such women to death. What do you say?" They said this to test him, so that they might have a charge against him.*

> *But Jesus bent down and began to write on the ground with his finger. When they persisted in questioning him, he straightened up and said to them, "Let the person among you who is without sin be the first to throw a stone at her." Then he bent down again and continued writing on the ground.*

*When they heard this, they went away one by one,
beginning with the oldest, and he was left alone with
the woman standing there. Then Jesus stood up and
said to her, "Woman, where are your accusers?
Hasn't anyone condemned you?" She said, "No one,
sir." Then Jesus said, "I don't condemn you either.
Go home, and from now on do not sin any
more"* (John 8: 2–12 *ff*).

Further discussion of the synagogue of Satan might
centre about the discussion raised by Paul in his letter to the
Romans. Who is the true Israel? Readers should wrestle with
Paul's analysis of the problem with Jewish salvation as the
apostle states this in Romans 9 – 11. Paul makes a distinction
about the Jews who are true Jews and those who are only
"genetic" Jews. To Paul, as with this passage in *Revelation*,
true Jews are those who recognize Jesus as Messiah, trust
him as Saviour, recognize him as the Son of God and honour
him as Sovereign Lord.

Most certainly "synagogue of Satan" is descriptive
of the Jewish treatment of Christians. In doing so they
compromised themselves by disobeying commandments
against falsifying their witness, breaking the Sabbath and
committing murder. Of course it was Satan's work and he
seemed to be ruler over the synagogue's teachings!

In keeping with the numerical codes, we suggest that
the term 10 days, connected with this church refers to a brief
period. It is not intended literally to be 10 days. If the
faithful of the church will continue in their faithfulness, they
shall receive a victor's reward – the laurel crown
(*stephonos*). The athletic or military victor was given the
crown, symbolic of life itself.

The scripture speaks of two deaths. The second death suggests complete separation from God. The contrast is with the death offered by Caesar's sword. Those persecuted may indeed be put to death. But they have been warned: the second death is far more punishing and permanent.

As this passage about Smyrna concludes it re-employs the formula used in each of the churches. The admonition is to know what the coded message says – the Holy Spirit will reveal it. Then too, it is a reminder to hear not only what is the specific message to this one church, but also the entire message that is intended for all the churches.

Smyrna's Report Card

Some matters were going well in Smyrna's church, despite its severe depression. The text says that the one who was slain at Calvary was raised on Easter. The text also says, *"First and Last died and came to life again."* He knew what his people were enduring. Jesus did not console them from an ivory tower. He was among fellow sufferers, *"a man of sorrows and acquainted with grief"* (Isaiah 53).

Here is a suggested summary of what Jesus was telling his church. God knows you are being tried by circumstances such as poverty, insults and testing. But remember Jesus who died and rose again. Christians are resurrection people, overcomers. Resurrection people live in hope because they know that ultimately God triumphs. Resurrection people keep on being faithful – for Jesus, the one who died and conquered death, continues being faithful to them. Resurrection people have a crown more worthy than the crowns of Cybele or Alexander the Great. The crown of eternal life lasts forever.

Athletic heroes won crowns when they were victorious. These were wreathes made of laurel leaves. When an Olympian won his race, the judge placed a myrtle or laurel wreath on his head. In some instances, a coin with an image of the hero was struck to honour him. Keep at it!

The city of Smyrna had died and been reborn. It had been incinerated previously but had rebuilt a magnificent municipality. Here is a signal that from human history there is hope. If that is true, then the one who died and lives again provides us with still more impressive hope that we will come through our difficulties with smiles and anticipation.

The text suggests that we may be killed but we cannot be obliterated. God has riches in his storehouse to give to those who hold fast and live triumphantly in the face of death itself. The believers in Smyrna knew little about personal riches but now Jesus was promising them wealth beyond measure – "*You are rich!*" They possessed God's wealth and it could never be taken from them.

CHAPTER FOUR

PERGAMUM

*"To the angel of the church in Pergamum write:
These are the words of him who has the sharp,
double-edged sword. I know where you live—where
Satan has his throne. Yet you remain true to my
name. You did not renounce your faith in me, not
even in the days of Antipas, my faithful witness, who
was put to death in your city—where Satan lives.
Nevertheless, I have a few things against you: There
are some among you who hold to the teaching of
Balaam, who taught Balak to entice the Israelites to
sin so that they ate food sacrificed to idols and
committed sexual immorality. Likewise, you also
have those who hold to the teaching of the
Nicolaitans. Repent therefore! Otherwise, I will soon
come to you and will fight against them with the*

67

sword of my mouth.
Whoever has ears, let them hear what the Spirit says
to the churches. To those who are victorious, I will
give some of the hidden manna. I will also give each
of them a white stone with a new name written on it,
known only to the one who receives it (Revelation
2:12–17).

When members of the church in Smyrna had copied
the letter sent from John as their own record, they bade
Godspeed to Prochorus as he left them for his subsequent
destination. Perhaps a traveling companion accompanied
Prochorus during the 85 kilometers' distance he hiked from
Symrna to Pergamum. They would have discussed the
agenda of persecution and faithful obedience that would
need to be the lot of believers.

Pergamum's Strategic Military Reality

Their route, unlike that from Ephesus to Smyrna,
first skirted the seacoast. About halfway to Pergamum, the
road took a sharp turn to the right and inland along the
Caicos River valley towards higher hill country. Possibly
their discussion included some of the history of their
destination, how once it was a city state, an empire in its
own right. Then it lost control and influence until it became a
shadow of its former self. Now it was relegated as one more
dot in the cities belonging to the Roman Empire.

One irony of the Roman subjugation of Pergamum
was that Attalus Eumenes had invited Rome to help him
defend his city against the tyrant Antiochus III. A few years
previous, Eumenes' father had protected the Greeks by
defending his territory against the Gauls (who had come to
the area as mercenaries of the king of Bithynia in 279 BC).

He stopped them in their tracks at his stronghold in Pergamum. This had helped to establish the district of Galatia, an area of the Hellenistic world that was relatively free from insurrections for a long period of time. But now, the Romans unquestionably were the rulers, the city-state bequeathed to them in 133 BC by a king (Attalus III) who distrusted his son.

Even as Prochorus entered Pergamum with the third sacred scroll, the city was waning in influence. Once the last eastern outpost of Greek civilization, once the capital of Asia, it had now to contend with rival cities like Ephesus and Symrna for commercial enterprise. In fact, soon Ephesus would earn the title, capital of Asia. Both these coastal cities fared better in commercial ventures because the sea routes under the *Pax Romana* guaranteed relative freedom from piracy or warfare. Trade and transportation routes which led through Pergamum began to lose their *raison d'etre* and therefore, their traffic, as Ephesus' prominent star began to rise.

Pergamum's Great Library

Prochorus and his possible Christian companion from Smyrna would have seen the hill of Pergamum from quite a distance. It was clearly visible because its stunning acropolis sits some 330 meters above the city. Its theatre (dedicated to Dionysus, deity of theatre and wine) of 80 rows held 10,000–15,000 spectators for its dramas. Pergamum was less complete in Prochorus' time than the ruins suggest today. The main reason for that is that construction continued some years after the biblical period. Yet Prochorus would have noted easily the significant library complex, above the acropolis of the city. It sat perched adjacent to the great temple to Athena, and slightly higher than the temple of Zeus.

King Attalus Eumenes II established the library in 196 BC. So famous was this library that it rivaled the great library of Alexandria. The name Pergamum was so linked to writing that it has permanently lived on in our language as the word "parchment." In Latin, the term for parchment was called *pergamena charta*, literally, "the paper of Pergamum." At its height, the library was said to contain 200,000 books, overshadowed only by Alexandria's library of 700,000 books. Marc Antony reduced the number of Pergamum's books (scrolls) by spiriting some of them to Alexandria to honour Cleopatra. Then he burned what he did not pillage.

In reality, parchment was not paper at all. It was animal skin that was dried and treated in a special way. The "books" were really scrolls, rolled between wooden spools. The derivation of the word parchment from Pergamum also has its own tale to tell. Apparently the Alexandrians were jealous of the Pergamene library. Alexandrians prevented their Pergamene rivals from the availability of papyrus for writing. It was then that the citizens of Pergamum invented parchment. When the Roman general and political personality Marc Antony seized Pergamum, he gave some of the Pergamene library to Alexandria. Thus its glory days concluded.

Pergamum's Health Centre

If Pergamum had authority as a strategic city militarily and commercially, it also had significance as a religious centre. Its religious dimensions were quite ecumenical, that is, coming from all over the world. The traditional oracles were important to the people of the city. In one famous instance, the king (Attalus I) used the internal organs of an animal sacrificed for omens, to assure his soldiers of victory against the mercenaries of Bithynia.

Pergamenes similarly celebrated some of the Egyptian gods. As the incidence of worship to Serapis increased, eventually a significant temple was erected in the city itself, in the lower city, not on the acropolis, to these Egyptian deities. The basilica (The Red Basilica) which was built just after the biblical period, later became a centre for emperor worship, and finally morphed into a basilica dedicated to Saint John.

At the edge of the Red Basilica is an entranceway to a kilometer-long tunnel that once connected the basilica to the Asklepion to the west. This is not the same tunnel that was used in therapy sessions at the famous healing centre itself.

Pergamum's Asklepion (various spellings) was world famous even before Galen's time (AD 131–210). Galen, a medical authority on the body's circulation and nervous systems, brought the "hospital" facility into even more international prominence. The cult of Aesklepios derived from worship of a mythological son of Apollo. According to legend, this mythical being learned great secrets of healing. So knowledgeable and wise was he that Zeus zapped him with lightning.

He was buried at Epidauros, where his cult continued through priests whom he himself taught and who now possessed healing abilities. The cult moved primarily from mainland Greece to the island of Kos, and then formed network centres throughout the Hellenistic world. There the priests practised insightful medicine. The snake was used as the symbol of Asklepios (var. Aesculapius), and therefore also its priests. Physicians still use that serpent symbol.

Hippocrates was the most famous of Asklepios' priests. Their centre at Kos, four centuries before Christ, provided new insights into epidemiology and fostered the basic medical ethics that are standards in medicine today. As we shall see when we discuss Laodicea, that city became a world famous centre for ophthalmology. Here in Pergamum, the focus was on the use of the mind in the work of healing. Pergamum's most famous medical priest was the aforementioned Galen, whose work in anatomy became widely recognized.

Entrance to the Asklepion was along the Sacred Road (*Via Tecta*) almost a kilometer long. Visitors today will note that parts of it were colonnaded, but that was an addition made during the reign of the emperor Hadrian (soon after the biblical period).

But much of the healing centre existed in the biblical period for the complex was begun in the 4th century BC, perhaps a century after Hippocrates' strong leadership in Kos. However, the "golden age" of the Asklepion was during Hadrian's period, somewhat after the writing of the book of *Revelation*.

Nonetheless, much of the Asklepion's medical therapy was contemporary with the New Testament period. Much was made of water and mud baths in the healing process. Relaxation was used to counter anxiety and stress. It has been learned that some of the water was radioactive.

When the patients entered the Asklepion for the first time, they removed their shoes and walked barefoot; they had been told that every step brought them closer to healing, further from death.

Primitive psychological methods were used effectively. Asklepion's priests created waterfalls to let their sound create an atmosphere for healing. Rest and relaxation were the order of the day. Uses of drugs, such as opium, were combined with the power of suggestion. As patients walked through a tunnel, doctor-priests hovered over openings in the tunnel ceiling to whisper words of encouragement or suggest, "You are getting better!"

This method was used by the French psychologist Émile Coué de Châtaigneraie who, in the late 19th and early 20th centuries introduced a method of psychotherapy and self-improvement based on optimistic autosuggestion. The Coué method is scarcely different from the techniques used in Pergamum.

Prayer to Asklepios was encouraged. Patients slept, often with the use of drug therapy, and were encouraged to reveal their dreams. The medical priests operated in such a way as to indicate healing and recovery. They then interpreted the dreams. The entire process was to affirm the well-being of each patient and to encourage their positive approach to life. The success rate was high but unlikely as high as its promoters wanted everyone to think.

However, since each patient who entered the healing centre was told that in no way could Hades (death) enter this healing centre, the power of suggestion worked its own kind of miracle. The entrance sign read, "IN THE NAME OF THE GODS, DEATH MAY NOT ENTER HERE."

Pagan Worship

Zeus was especially honoured in Pergamum by Eumenes II's construction of a formidable temple in 190 BC. Greek myths proclaim that he was born there. Since Zeus was the top deity in Greek mythology – a sort of executive god – he received top honours in Greek temple building. Pergamum's priests presiding over the prominent Zeus temple made certain that the populace fully recognized and venerated the deity.

The Zeus sanctuary had celebrity status in the city, superintending the society below. Evidently, priests who were placed beneath the main altar could create smoke and maneuver the idol so that the image appeared to be alive. The people would tremble at this authority. The vestiges of the temple (except its base which remains in Pergamum) are now located in a Berlin Museum, its altar fully reconstructed. Jesus' words noted this temple as "the throne of Satan."

Religious activities were not limited to the worship of Asklepios, of course. Undoubtedly the city itself had many places of worship and many gods to indwell them. The main and most obvious worship centre was high above the city at the acropolis.

One feature of the religious mosaic practised in Pergamum was the temple of Cybele. As we noted earlier in Smyrna, Cybele, as stated previously, was the "mother goddess" of Phrygia in Anatolia. It was originally believed that she came to earth as a meteorite. A temple to her honour was built here in this city and named the Megalesion. For a year it held a meteorite that was deemed to represent the goddess, and then the king sent the idol to Rome to ensure victory of the Romans over the Carthaginians.

A temple to Dionysius was also part of the acropolis' religious scenario. Dionysius (Bacchus) was god of wine and nature. Dionysius was also related to the drama activities of Greek society and a very large amphitheater, quite evident to Prochorus long before he entered the city, was prominently built into the sunset side of the acropolis.

The complex of buildings called the "tenemos" of Demeter indicates that Demeter too was a major religious force in this city. Demeter was among the goddesses of Olympus. Her charge was to guard the vegetation and to prosper marriage.

We have not mentioned Athena. Athena was acclaimed by a very large temple that sat between the Pergamene Library and the temple of Zeus. It was easily seen from its vantage point overlooking the city from the southern edge of the city's acropolis. Athena's temple adjacent to the great library may have been a link that reading and wisdom (Athena's specialty) go well together.

Pergamum's Report Card

What of Christ's Church set in this historical city rife with pagan worship? What account does it give for itself? Has it been, or is it a beacon of light for the gospel? This question is one to be asked of any church in the midst of a public darkness where Christ's light can shine for good.

The letter to Pergamum is largely complimentary to the Christians who inhabit the city. Jesus knows that a dark paganism surrounds them in the form of pagan worship, i.e.,

Satan's throne. He knows that the precious name of Jesus has not been sullied by apostasy in the midst of persecution. These believers have "held fast" to his character by living like Jesus and living for Jesus. Some, like Antipas, had shed their life blood rather than bow their heads to any of the pagan deities or to the emperor who claimed he was divine.

Despite the high praise Jesus afforded this church, he noted some black marks in its membership. A few members of the Christian community lived a double life. They held to a faith in Jesus while participating in pagan rituals. Paul counseled the Roman church that worse things could happen than to die for one's faith. *"If we have been united with him in a death like his, we will certainly also be united with him in a resurrection like his"* (Romans 6:5).

The exalted Jesus cited Balaam (Numbers 22:1 to 24:25) who symbolized concession and conformity to avoid martyrdom. Christian faith cannot contain compromised character. Paul made this abundantly apparent to Christians in Corinth. The followers of Nicolas in Pergamum also failed the test of Christian character as they did in Smyrna.

> *Food does not bring us near to God; we are no worse if we do not eat, and no better if we do. Be careful, however, that the exercise of your rights does not become a stumbling block to the weak. For if anyone with a weak conscience sees you, with all your knowledge, eating in an idol's temple, won't they be emboldened to eat what is sacrificed to idols? So this weak brother or sister, for whom Christ died, is destroyed by your knowledge When you sin against them in this way and wound their weak conscience, you sin against Christ* (1 Corinthians 8:8–13).

It was not too late to reverse the failures. Jesus requires the miscreants to repent of their compromises and apostasy. He promises to meet with them. Jesus implores the entire church to reject this sin in their midst and to return to their true faith. The Church cannot accept members who are untrue to the Christ of the gospels.

Jesus promised Pergamum's church several things. One was manna from heaven. In their wilderness wandering the people of Israel experienced a daily ration of manna, a kind of bread. It was given in quantity enough for one day at a time. As John wrote about the Lord, *"I am the bread of heaven"* (John 6:32). Jesus was promising that just as the Israelites were attended by God during their long sojourn, so the Church would be nourished by God in the present era. Manna represents spiritual food and life. The ones who refuse to eat the forbidden fruit of idol worship and its accompanying indulgent love feasts and sexual orgies, will be protected by and provided for by Jesus.

Jesus also promised the Pergamum faithful a white stone. White and black stones were common in the area. Black basalt stones were the product of volcanic action and erosion. White stones were silica or gypsum resulting from deposits. You see them, black and white, along the beaches of Turkey and Greece.

White represented honour and hospitality. White stones were used as admissions to theatres or to those acquitted in trials. The white stones represented victory. Perhaps the name on the white stone is that of Jesus himself. Perhaps it is intended to follow the familiar pattern of renaming people or cities when rebuilt or conquered by a

77

general. Perhaps it is like Napoleon's action of renaming his conquered citizens after the occupations they plied in their daily lives. Whatever the name on the stones means, they are a positive gift to conquerors from the Saviour.

The traditional injunction repeated to each church complete the judgment offered by Christ. *"He who has an ear, let him hear what the Spirit says to the churches."* Since the judgment was read aloud, all who were present for the reading could hear it. It includes all the churches, every church. So it means, "Now hear this. The Holy Spirit is talking to *you* individually and collectively. And *you*. And *you*." *Ad infinitum*.

CHAPTER FIVE

THYATIRA

"To the angel of the church in Thyatira write:
These are the words of the Son of God, whose eyes
are like blazing fire and whose feet are like
burnished bronze. I know your deeds, your love and
faith, your service and perseverance, and that you
are now doing more than you did at first.
Nevertheless, I have this against you: You tolerate
that woman Jezebel, who calls herself a prophet. By
her teaching she misleads my servants into sexual
immorality and the eating of food sacrificed to
idols. I have given her time to repent of her
immorality, but she is unwilling. So I will cast her
on a bed of suffering, and I will make those who
commit adultery with her suffer intensely, unless
they repent of her ways. I will strike her children
dead. Then all the churches will know that I am he
who searches hearts and minds, and I will repay
each of you according to your deeds. Now I say to
the rest of you in Thyatira, to you who do not hold
to her teaching and have not learned Satan's so-
called deep secrets, 'I will not impose any other
burden on you, except to hold on to what you have

until I come.'
To those who are victorious and do my will to the
end, I will give authority over the nations — they
'will rule them with an iron scepter and will dash
them to pieces like pottery' — just as I have
received authority from my Father. I will also give
them the morning star. Whoever has ears, let them
h e a r   w h a t   t h e   S p i r i t   s a y s   t o   t h e
churches" (Revelation 2: 18–29).

In his book *Revelation as Drama* (p. 37) James L.
Blevins introduces us to his fictional mayor of Thyatira,
Lactanius. A good politician and protector of his city's
importance, the mayor says, "Welcome to our city. Thyatira
is thought by some to be the least important of the seven
cities, because it is a workingman's town. We feel it is quite
important."

The mayor is spot on. The city had considerable
importance for many reasons. It produced wealth for the
area. It served as a shield for Pergamum in case of attack. It
served as a conduit for trade from several directions. The
city was situated on a Roman Imperial Post Road. Today's
Turkish city of Akhisar surrounds the ruins of what was
Thyatira. The modern city of 20,000 inhabitants still favours
the textile trade. Thyatira was a unionized community.

The Buffer Zone

Like the working class it housed, the city was used
and abused by the more sophisticated Pergamum. Thyatira,
almost 70 kilometers southeast of Pergamum was a useful
buffer in case of attack aimed at the greater city. Thus it gave
ample warning to Pergamum a distance away of any possible
or impending disaster. This distance gave time to alert

Pergamum's defences to be in place. The aristocrats in Pergamum found it convenient that the working class citizens of Thyatira could soften the danger of any invading force whoever that might be.

Unlike Pergamum, Thyatira was constructed on level ground. Despite the apocryphal Mayor Lactanius' plea, Thyatira was an unimpressive city. It's current city of Akhisar is likewise unimposing today. It is a convenient 15-minute all-purpose bus pause on the road from Istanbul to Izmir.

Thyatira's situation, however, enhanced its development of crafts, for its manufactured products were easily transported southeast through the Philadelphia region or northeast to the Sea of Marmara and Rome's great military highway, the Egnatian Way. Trade was also routed west to Smyrna or any port along the Mediterranean Sea.

In the biblical book of Acts (chapter 16), author Luke's account tells of Lydia was who baptized in the Gangites River coursing gently from north to south through Philippi. Lydia's presence in Philippi also suggests that she joined a small group of Jews and God-fearers in regular participation of worship at the Gangites riverbank.

The riparian-setting worship venue suggests it was a suitable place of ritual purification for Jews and prospective proselytes. Luke describes Lydia as a "seller of purple," i.e., from Thyatira, a merchant importing and exporting textiles made in her native city.

The hint in Acts is that she was a well-to-do woman.

Lydia was domiciled in a house with guest rooms for people like Paul and Silas and accommodation for her "household," probably her servants. Maybe textile dealers stopped there overnight. The presence of the textile dealer Lydia in Philippi reveals much about the far-reaching trading practices of Thyatira. Diaspora Jews took to crafts like textiles or sold them because they did not have a major connection with the worship of pagan deities in Greece or Asia. At least Lydia, as a sales agent, may have been immune from pagan rites.

Anyone would be curious about the possibility that Lydia, the first convert to Christ's gospel in Europe, was also the missionary who returned home to evangelize her native town. While nothing is beyond possibility, that notion cannot easily be set aside.

Myriad Deities

Thyatira was a magnet for clothiers, cutters, smiths, potters, bankers, slavers, leather-workers, idol-makers and dyers. These trades were proud of their craftsmanship. They sought good reputations for the quality of their work. Workmanship was important not only to their individual reputations, but to the entire Thyatiran community. They demanded that the entire guild be respected and supported by every member. Moreover, productive workmanship honoured the pagan deities associated as patrons, guardians and protectors of their specific guild.

The cult of the divine Caesar was well-established by this time. Nero worship was underway in Thyatira also. By the time Domitian was emperor, adoration of the emperor was mandatory. A hint of this is found in chapter 13, where in code, emperor worship from Rome is thinly disguised as Babylon, and the whore who sat on seven hills (17:9) is identified with the number 666. Rome had seven hills, not Babylon. The number 666 is the symbol of incompleteness, i.e., absolute evil. Caesar Nero, using an alphabet with Hebrew equivalent numbering, adds up to 666. Message: do not worship Caesar. Caesar is the beast!

Thyatira's main deity was Apollo, the sun god. His job was to raise the sun in the morning, carry the sun across the sky and set it for the night. Greek mythology explains that Apollo had a love/hate relationship with Zeus, the executive God, but we will avoid pursuing that tangent.

Apollo also had some human agents, namely, oracles. These oracles, women, prophesied the future. The mythical figure Tyrimnos represented Apollo in Thyatira. His image was on its coins. He was pictured on a fighting steed wielding an axe in one hand and a laurel wreath in the other. These were symbols of protection and healing.

Thyatira's name means "the castle of Thya or Thea." That description suggests a female deity of some sort, *thea* being the Greek word for goddess. A temple of Tyrimnos gave the entrance to the city a status and proposed a respect that anyone entering the city was obliged to note. Tyrimnos was a priest of Apollo. Note: Apollo guarded this city! Christians knew better. The God who made the sun, moon and stars, who provided salvation through Jesus, Son of God, Saviour, Lord of lords and King of kings – he was in control of Thyatira.

As noted, sibyls were present in Thyatira and one particular sibyl had a name – Sambatha. She was an oracle (prophetess) of Pythian Apollo. The word Pythian derives from python, the serpent, who was deemed, like an owl, to possess great wisdom. Apollo, goes the myth, slew Pytho and his body slipped into the cracks at Delphi's Apollo temple. The fumes of Pytho's decaying body rose from the crevices. These vapours provided wisdom and prophetic knowledge for Delphi's oracles.

We meet such a sibyl in Philippi (Acts 16), where Paul casts the evil spirit out of the young woman. At the great temple of Pythian Apollo in Delphi, Greece, such oracles were consulted with frequency to predict important matters, such as whether a king should go to war. Sometimes, such local sibyls were free-lancers.

More often sibyls were slaves whose owners made a healthy living out of offering them to make predictions for curious merchants, such as Lydia who wondered where the trade winds might blow. In Revelation 2:20, Jezebel calls herself a prophet. Is this a connection to Apollo? Probably!

Thyatira then, is a lunch bucket community where workers "brown bagged" their noon meal. Think Pittsburgh PA or Hamilton ON or Sydney Mines NS when you think of Thyatira. Thyatira went hand in hand with guilds. Guilds established the prices for their goods. They acted as a marketing board. They set the standards for gold, for example. Guilds decided on the requirements of apprentices Guilds constantly sought new markets. They were always on the lookout for new threats to their clientele. Guilds provided an upward mobility for some members who were elected to guild governorship. Guilds also provided social networking, a form of U-tube, Facebook or Twitter.

Guilds and Their Patrons

Each guild held its meeting when the days' work was over, not every day of course. Guilds, like many modern unions, provided incentives to better production, emphasis on quality, training sessions, encouragement, or comparison to other successful workers' enterprises.

However, the bottom line was that the guild deity, usually a name associated with Apollo, needed honouring or placating, for the success of the guild. Neglect the deity and business would drop off. The implications for Christians are enormous. How could one be free from accident or poor health if the benefactor was not properly honoured? How could commerce grow, or competition be overcome if the patron was not placated?

Guild meetings usually focused upon veneration of the guild's patron deity. Each guild meeting was separate from another but the formula was similar. For each meeting, the membership attended to promote the patron's pristine reputation. That was paramount. Guild members could not assume their association with their spiritual sponsor or take it for granted.

Worship often consisted of sacrificing animals or birds to the idol, the food becoming dinner for the attending members. Those joining the gathering poured out token libations to the false god or goddess and drank the remainder of the wine as their tribute to him or her. They got drunk.

Often, the guild meetings ended in a sexual orgy. Union with a sibyl or a priestess became communion with the guild's patron god. One can note how this practice became a specific issue in Corinth's church. Atop the mountain outside Corinth, the Acrocorinth, Aphrodite's thousand cult priestesses acted as temple prostitutes.

Some of them accepted Jesus as Saviour and ceased their prostitution. As Paul said, *"such were some of you"* (1:6:11) when he wrote to the congregation in Corinth. Other temple priestesses may have drifted into the public worship services in Corinth and expressed their opinions. That may be why Paul instructed Corinthian church leaders; *"women should be silent in the church"* (1:14:34).

Ergo, required attendance at such a guild event became more that problematical for Christians. There was no room for compromise. If an animal was to be sacrificed at the start of the guild assembly, Christians might be tardy in arriving. Some of them might avoid eating the food that had been sacrificed to an idol.

If sexual intercourse with the guild's cult priestesses followed the libations, Christians left the assembly early. Guild members would notice that the Christians tended to arrive late and leave early and some did not eat with them.

This left the guild's non-believers wondering if the patron deity was pleased, or if such absences affected their livelihood. Translate that into real time. It meant that guild members were suspicious, if not very irked, perhaps retributional at Christians who would not toe the guild line of pagan responsibilities. They were failing their other guild members, were they not? They were becoming isolationists instead of being guild team members.

Secret IDs in Thyatira

Scripture names certain people or images that relate to this particular city. The code words are: *Son of God*; *blazing fire and burnished brass*; *Jezebel*; *iron and pottery*; *Satan's secrets*; and *morning star*. Other words like "good works," "service," "patient endurance" and "love" are keys to understand this church. Factor in the "guild-oriented" city and they become more significant. None of these are too difficult to translate – except to Roman censors, perhaps.

An iron scepter and broken pottery reflect both the ironworkers' guild and the potters' guild in Thyatira. The rod used by Israel's poet in Psalm 23 is a gentle rod to herd sheep and stabilize a shepherd's gait. However, the rod mentioned in this section of *Revelation* chapter two is stiff and authoritative. Iron rods easily destroy pottery.

Broken pottery is a potter's nightmare. Shattered shards reflect imperfection in their making. Potters will not sell their imperfections. They soon cast them off and will not reuse them. They are good for nothing but the trash heap.

These words are connected to Psalm 2 which speaks to the authority of Messiah over the earth's nations.

> *You will break them with a rod of iron;*
> *you will dash them to pieces like pottery."*
> *Therefore, you kings, be wise;*

be warned, you rulers of the earth.
Serve the Lord with fear
and celebrate his rule with trembling.

"Son of God" compares Jesus with Apollo, son of Zeus. Eyes like blazing fire and feet like burnished bronze (comparing Jesus to Apollo) also factor into the images of Apollo the sun deity. Moreover, these images ring true with the smithy's guild in Thyatira. This is the only occasion in which "Son of God" is used in *Revelation*, so its meaning is clear.

Jezebel is reference to the spouse of Ahab, king of Israel (1 Kings 16:31.32). She enticed the people of Israel away from YHWH to follow the Canaanite deity adored in Sidon, her native city. It was an abomination to the LORD, partly because it broke the commandment to have no other gods before YAHWEH, and partly because it was adulation connected with cultic sexual prostitution. The affiliation of Jezebel as a sybil adds to the infamy of the name. No parents call their daughters by the name of Jezebel – that is how offensive her name is. Yet a Jezebel was alive and active in Thyatira.

What is Satan's deep secret? This epithet relates to some Christians who resisted the concept of Jesus' full divinity and full humanity. Gnosticism was prevalent in Asia Minor and became a heresy that severely afflicted the Church. Jesus would have none of it! Gnostics believed that true knowledge of God came through a special inner knowledge that they alone understood. So they discounted behaviour as unimportant and inconsequential. Thus they could "sin" while holding onto the inner knowledge they believed God had given them. They mistook the depths of evil for the deep things of God.

The morning star is a sign of dawn, a new day, and a new age. It is the age of the risen Jesus, resurrected, ascended and glorified. Persecution may severely inflict believers but they have a hope exceeding their earthly agony.

"Good works" has a double entendre. It refers both to the quality of workmanship with which the guilds were proud; it refers to the way in which Thyatira's Christians carried out kind deeds in a loving way throughout their community. In more modern times, the early Anabaptist Hutterites believed that the high quality of their work was an evangelical message of the gospel for its own sake. Thyatira's believers were patient, awaiting God's ultimate redemption. They demonstrated love to each other in charitable deeds of kindness.

The Thyatiran Report Card

Christians in this fourth church received a creditable mark. They patiently awaited Jesus' full promises. They kept their faith. They performed deeds of good works. They were kind and loving.

Sometimes rough and crude people do not receive our love. We ostracize them because of their crude language and curt responses. This applies both to "working class" people and executives. Each can be hard to love. Sometimes they feel exploited and misunderstood.

However, some of the church's membership required the discipline of their tough love. Love sometimes requires "toughness." "*You can't serve God and mammon*," Jesus told his listeners in his Sermon on the Mount (Matthew 6:24). You cannot have God and Ba'al.

Faith is not always found in crusty, hard-nosed workers. One can often find grievances among them. "Service," described as a virtue by Jesus in the Thyatira passage, is difficult for some of the lunch bucket crowd. They toil hard all day; shouldn't they earn a rest for their aching bones when their daily work is finished? Should teachers in schools take on volunteer Sunday School teaching when they work so hard all week? Should textile workers spend their "leisure" hours making clothes for widows and their children?

"Patient endurance" is likewise a Christian virtue that is hard to capture. The Thyatira throng worked for the equivalent of hourly wages. They were not accustomed to long range planning. They preferred instant results. They echoed a common theme which reverberates through the centuries, "We want it and we want it now."

God does not allow worship that includes Ba'alism as an acceptable second option. Jezebels everywhere must wholly be rooted out of church fellowship. Is not cancer exorcised from a body so that the body may heal? That's what Jesus was telling believers in Thyatira. Or can the church deal with the matter in a more accommodating way?

How does a church deal with immorality in its midst? Should Christians be harsh and expunge the adulterer from its midst? Should they be merciful and offer no reproach at all, as if it was not their business? If believers sever their connection with the offender, who will minister to that individual?

Moreover, Jesus is willing to forgive Jezebel's disciples if they repent and mend their ways. Jesus refers to the Church as the "bride of Christ" (Revelation 22:17). The bride must not be sullied by less than chaste deportment.

An issue familiar to most "union" shops arose in Thyatira. Union shops are often closed. A member, upon joining, pays his dues and cannot opt out. Sometimes the union takes a stance that is contrary to the beliefs of an individual member. Not only is a union like that, but so are associations we join in which executives speak on behalf of members. AARP or CARP (organizations which purport to speak on behalf of retired persons in the USA and Canada) often lobby governments on legislation. Not all members are happy with the stance the associations make. What to do?

This was the dilemma of Christians in Thyatira's guilds. They needed the solidarity of the guilds for their security and income. Yet, they wanted to opt out of some practices conflicting with their core beliefs. The issue continues in every society.

CHAPTER SIX

SARDIS

"To the angel of the church in Sardis write:

These are the words of him who holds the seven spirits of God and the seven stars. I know your deeds; you have a reputation of being alive, but you are dead. Wake up! Strengthen what remains and is about to die, for I have found your deeds unfinished in the sight of my God.
Remember, therefore, what you have received and heard; hold it fast, and repent. But if you do not wake up, I will come like a thief, and you will not know at what time I will come to you.
Yet you have a few people in Sardis who have not soiled their clothes. They will walk with me, dressed in white, for they are worthy. Those who are victorious will, like them, be dressed in white. I will never blot out their names from the book of life, but will acknowledge their names before my Father and his angels. Whoever has ears, let them hear what the Spirit says to the churches" (Revelation 3:1–6).

After Prochorus left his fourth scroll of *The Revelation of Jesus Christ* in Thyatira, he gathered the remaining three documents and headed to Sardis. It was a two-day hike at the best of circumstances, over 33 (52 kms.) miles southeast of Thyatira or 45 miles (70 kms.) east of Smyrna. That Sardis was situated on major trade routes meant that the postman of Patmos could find appropriate places to eat and sojourn overnight. Perhaps he also visited believers who were scattered along the route. He would leave one of the three remaining scrolls in Sardis.

A Sardis History

Christians who witnessed for their Lord Jesus in the city of Sardis lived in a community well-known in ancient history. Its fame spread throughout the Assyrian empire. At one time, it exchanged ambassadors with the well-known emperor Ashurbanipal. At one time, Sardis was the capital of the kingdom of Lydia (which may be where the seller of purple mentioned in Acts 16 got her name).

In its heyday in the 8th century BC, Lydia earned a reputation for manufacturing. Perhaps some of that fame derived from Thyatira's industries of many guilds. Among the manufacturing was the weaving of carpets and renowned for dyes especially in wool used for the carpets. The city was not without disaster. Persians, Athenian Greeks and Romans captured it.

After the city's unwelcome sacking and burning by Athens, the vulnerable metropolis rebuilt. In the attack, Athenians had destroyed the temple honouring Cybele, the

Phrygian version of Artemis. Cybele was a fertility symbol and its temple replete with cultic prostitutes. Because it was the token of successful living, Sardis' leaders quickly rebuilt Cybele's temple to safeguard the affluent achievements of their city. In AD 17 an earthquake leveled the city of Sardis. The city rebuilt again. After AD 313 Constantine moved his capital from Rome to Constantinople. He built new roads in Lydia, bypassed Sardis and relegated the city to a much lesser role.

The Gold Standard

At one time also, Sardis was the richest city in the world and was dubbed "the golden city." The most famous of Sardis' kings was the wealthy Crœssus. He lived from 595 BC to about 547 BC. His reputation was worldwide and grew every time his biography was retold of the gold he possessed. Some of it is factual. Some is recorded in the annals of the historian Herodotos. He was most fortunate in obtaining the gold. It likely came from small nuggets – "golden sands" – in the nearby Pactolus River which ran adjoining the temple of Aphrodite, immediately at the base of Cyrus' acropolis on Mount Tmolus. He did not have to win his gold in battle.

Crœssus was the first to mint gold coins, crude at first. They were made of an amalgam of gold and silver called electrum. Likely he was the first to refine gold. He used the seed of the carob (circa 200 mg) or locust bean tree to measure the weight of his gold. "Carob" became "carat" and carat has continued as the standard measure of jewelry.

The gold translated into battle, however. The wealth attracted emperor Cyrus the Great, who busied himself enlarging his realm. Crœssus traveled to Delphi to seek counsel from the oracle of Pythian Apollo and to ensure its accuracy, generously paid for and sought the additional advice of the oracle Amphiaraus (a seer honoured by both Zeus and Apollo). The oracles, whose answers were always ambiguous, told Crœssus that if he attacked the Persians he would destroy an empire. Crœssus proved that we believe what we want to hear. Crœssus attacked Cyrus and destroyed his own kingdom.

We meet Cyrus in the biblical book of *Nehemiah*. His respect for religions of those he conquered provided the means for Nehemiah and other Jews to return from captivity to their homeland to rebuild the walls of Jerusalem. Cyrus appears to be a form of messiah, one anointed of the Lord. Isaiah writes of him (Isaiah 45:1–4),

> *This is what the Lord says to his anointed, to Cyrus, whose right hand I take hold of to subdue nations before him and to strip kings of their armour, to open doors before him so that gates will not be shut: I will go before you and will level the mountains; I will break down gates of bronze and cut through bars of iron.*
>
> *I will give you the treasures of darkness, riches stored in secret places, so that you may know that I am the Lord, the God of Israel, who summons you by name. For the sake of Jacob my servant, of Israel my*

chosen, I summon you by name and bestow on you a
title of honour, though you do not acknowledge me.

Cyrus' end time came soon enough. He lost a major
naval battle with the Greeks at Salamis in the Aegean, and
retreated to his homeland. Then, in a battle with Egyptian
forces, he lost his life. At that point, the Greeks became the
dominant world power. When Alexander the Great swept
through Persian territory, he stopped at Sardis and ordered
that a new temple be built, one to Artemis. Time has covered
it with sand but excavations have revealed it to have
magnificent design. At the base of its remaining columns are
decorations of arrows and eggs, symbols of death and
fertility.

Slacking Sentinels

Crœssus' acropolis fortress atop Mount Tmolus was
practically impregnable. Or so he thought. One side of the
hill was so precipitous that no one assumed to guard it. The
view from the watchtower fortress provided Crœssus and his
sentinels with an unobstructed commanding view of military
and trade traffic along adjacent roads of the Hermus Valley.

Hyerœaedes, a Mede, led Emperor Cyrus' army into
Sardis. His siege lasted on and off nearly two years with a
winter vacation for the army of Cyrus. The story is told that
the emperor offered a reward to any soldier who gained
entrance to the city. One day a soldier noted that a sentinel
atop the acropolis dropped his helmet. The soldier noticed
the path he took to retrieve the helmet. The Mede leader

dispatched some solders that took the same route into the stronghold, surprising the Sardian solders. The forces of Cyrus quickly overtook the city and captured Crœssus. That story, whether fact or fiction, became a well remembered highly embossed footnote on Sardis. The watchmen failed to watch!

Crœssus fate was sealed at that point. Other stories followed, apocryphal or factual. Cyrus sought to kill Crœssus. He taunted the Sardian king. "See, my soldiers are looting your treasures." Crœssus replied, "My treasures? They're your treasures now. Your troops are thieving you." The looting stopped.

Nonetheless, Cyrus decided to put an end to Crœssus. He bound the king and put him on a pyre, then lit the wood. Saddened by what he was doing to someone he regarded as a "good man," suggests one account, Cyrus' servants attempted to douse the flames but they could not. Crœssus allegedly prayed to Apollo who sent a heavy rain to extinguish the fire. Historians place no credence in the myth of Crœssus' deliverance and believe that Crœssus met his end there and then. Cyrus' conquest occurred about 547 or 546 BC.

Stuttering History

This writer once had a professor who pointed out that, "history repeats itself so often you'd think it was stuttering." Failed watchcare surfaced again in 216 BC. This time, it was Antiochus the Great who stormed the fortress on the top of Mount Tmolus. Once more, vigilance was the issue. Antiochus attacked Sardis' stronghold when the guards showed their complacency. Antiochus' army scaled the ramparts and subjugated the citizens.

The Greek historian Polybius (220–146 BC), a contemporary of Antiochus the Great wrote about the king's victory over Sardis. Polybius detailed specific actions, a few of which appear as follows:

> Lagoras the Cretan . . . had considerable military experience, and had observed that as a rule the strongest cities are those which most easily fall into the hands of the enemy owing to the negligence of their inhabitants when, relying on the natural and artificial strength of a place, they omit to keep guard and become generally remiss. He had also noticed that these very cities are usually captured at their very strongest points where the enemy [is] supposed to regard attack as hopeless. At present he saw that owing to the prevailing notion of the extreme strength of Sardis, every one despaired of taking it by any such *coup de main*, and that their only hope was to subdue it by famine; and this made him pay all the more attention to the matter and seek out every possible means in his eagerness to get hold of some such favourable opportunity. Observing that the wall along the so-called Saw — which connects the citadel with the town — was unguarded, he began to entertain schemes and hopes of availing himself of this. He had discovered the remissness of the guard here from the following circumstance. The place is exceedingly precipitous and beneath it there is a ravine into which they used to throw the corpses from the city and the entrails of the horses and mules that died, so that a quantity of vultures and other birds used to collect here. Lagoras, then, seeing that when the birds had eaten their fill they used constantly to rest on the cliffs and on the wall, knew

99

for a certainty that the wall was not guarded and was usually deserted. He now proceeded to visit the ground at night and note carefully at what places ladders could be brought up and placed against the wall. Having found that this was possible at a certain part of the cliff, he approached the king on the subject. The king welcomed the proposal, and begged Lagoras to put his design in execution . . . (*The Histories of Polybius*, book IV, 15).

Antiochus also moved some hundreds of Jews from Mesopotamia to Sardis as a hedge against any possible Phrygian rebellion. Thus a synagogue existed in the city when John penned Jesus' words to the city. More than a century later, an elaborate Synagogue building was erected on the plain at Sardis. It mirrored the reality that Jews prospered in that city. The excavated Synagogue ruins are adjoined to a large building once dedicated to the Roman emperor who was worshipped as a divinity in this place.

Sardian Deities

As noted, Greek deities played a major role in the rulers and citizens of Sardis. Apollo held top place in the hearts and minds of Sardians. Evidence of this is in Crœssus' readiness to consult oracles in far-away Delphi. Apollo was connected to Asklepios, deity of healing, and to Aphrodite, deity of fertility.

When Alexander the Great rolled through the area, he funded the erection of a temple to Artemis, the ruins of which have been excavated. Artemis was also a fertility deity, highly respected throughout Lydia and especially esteemed in Ephesus as has been noted. Later, when Tiberius funded a reconstruction of Sardis after an earthquake, he ensured that a temple was built to Cybele (another form of a fertility cult).

Not all deities worshipped in Sardis were of Greek mythology. Judaism, brought by transplants from Babylon or by traders within Asia Minor, saw to it that the God of Abraham, Isaac and Jacob was honoured in the keeping of commandments and rituals. How well the Jewish population mixed with Christians is unknown. In Smyrna they clashed.

Coded Words

"*Wake up!*" This is a call to the sentries who kept the gates of the church in Sardis. Crœssus' soldiers had slacked off in their duty. It was a history lesson for the church. Someone, some people, in the Sardian church had fallen asleep at the switch and the church had derailed. Qin Shi Huang built the initial part of the Great Wall of China to keep out northern invaders. He forgot that the gatekeepers could be bribed.

Crœssus thought that sentries would protect him from anyone trying to scale the acropolis of Sardis but he did not calculate their ennui or factor in their apathy. The church needed a wake-up call and this letter provided it. How can the church be prepared to face evil if the church is snoozing? How can the church prepare for the coming of the Lord if it is asleep? Heed Peter's words:

> *But do not forget this one thing, dear friends: With the Lord a day is like a thousand years, and a thousand years are like a day. The Lord is not slow*

in keeping his promise, as some understand slowness. Instead he is patient with you, not wanting anyone to perish, but everyone to come to repentance. But the day of the Lord will come like a thief. The heavens will disappear with a roar; the elements will be destroyed by fire, and the earth and everything done in it will be laid bare.

Since everything will be destroyed in this way, what kind of people ought you to be? You ought to live holy and godly lives as you look forward to the day of God and speed its coming. That day will bring about the destruction of the heavens by fire, and the elements will melt in the heat. But in keeping with his promise we are looking forward to a new heaven and a new earth, where righteousness dwells (1 Peter 3:8–13).

"*Seven stars*" represent the collective pastors of the seven churches who are messengers of the gospel. They look out for their parishioners and seek to keep them keen on their faith. They are responsible to Jesus himself who entrusts them with the care of his believers. "*Seven spirits*" is another way of referring to the completeness of the Holy Spirit's oversight.

"*I know*" is Jesus' way of telling his church that God keeps an eye on them. "*He will bring to light what is hidden in darkness and will expose the motives of people's hearts. At that time each will receive their praise from God*" (1 Corinthians 4:5). God is not blind to the affairs of the Church. Jesus is there to instruct his followers every time the truth must be told. "Dr." Jesus, the Great Physician, has diagnosed his church and has provided a summary of both a verdict and prescription.

"Keep that," refers to those who have strayed form the gospel. But Jesus points them back to the gospel they first knew. He bids them repent and then keep or preserve the initial faith they once embraced. As a noun, "keep" has another meaning. A keep is the most impregnable part of a citadel. Christian Sardians are by faith, instructed to preserve the salvation provided by Jesus' atonement and secure it in the most protected part of their minds and bodies.

"Strengthen what remains," is a telling phrase. It suggests that most of the church is dead wrong but a few of that number are still very much alive. False Christians are toxic to the entire body. Believers must trust the saving Lord to provide antibodies for the rabid infection virulent in the church.

Moral turpitude was rife in Sardis but Jesus called some believers as "Worthy" of his name. The clothing they wear is not soiled, but pure white, reflecting their spiritual and moral goodness. Those who conquer their bent to sin will also be rewarded with white garments. White clothing represents the ability and willingness of Jesus to forgive and to save. The church is reminded to ponder that great truth. *My dear children, you come from God and belong to God. You have already won a big victory over those false teachers, for the Spirit in you is far stronger than anything in the world* (1 John 4:4 MSG).

Jesus promises to confess the name of worthy church members before his Father. Name is important to the ancients, especially to Jews and Christians. Name represents character. God allowed his "name" to dwell in Zion, which meant both his presence and his holiness. We pray, "in Jesus' name." So when Jesus offers to tell the name of worthy believers to the Father, it is Jesus' affirmation that such people merit God's eternal blessings. Names cannot be taken lightly and must be respected. Listen to Solomon asking God to indwell the temple he had built for him so that God's character would abide among the people of Judah and Israel:

> But will God really dwell on earth? The heavens, even the highest heaven, cannot contain you. How much less this temple I have built! Yet give attention to your servant's prayer and his plea for mercy, Lord my God. Hear the cry and the prayer that your servant is praying in your presence this day. May your eyes be open toward this temple night and day, this place of which you said, 'My Name shall be there,' so that you will hear the prayer your servant prays toward this place. Hear the supplication of your servant and of your people Israel when they pray toward this place. Hear from heaven, your dwelling place, and when you hear, forgive (1 Kings 8:27–30).

Sardis' Church Report Card

The church at Sardis is in trouble with God. It had become complacent and apathetic. It took little heed to watch and pray so as to not fall into temptation. Had not Jesus taught his followers to be watchful and alert? Watchfulness is required against temptation for one thing. It is also required for preparation awaiting Jesus' return to conclude human history.

Neither smugness nor self-satisfaction are acceptable traits among any believers and in any congregation. Watchfulness caused Sardis to fall to Cyrus in the mid-6th century BC and again to Antiochus III in a later century. Sardis was careless about it treasures and its resources.

"Therefore keep watch, because you do not know on what day your Lord will come. But understand this: If the owner of the house had known at what time of night the thief was coming, he would have kept watch and would not have let his house be broken into. So you also must be ready, because the Son of Man will come at an hour when you do not expect him. Who then is the faithful and wise servant, whom the master has put in charge of the servants in his household to give them their food at the proper time? It will be good for that servant whose master finds him doing so when he returns" (Matthew 24:42–46).

Sardis had become a ho-hum church. Many among its membership lacked interest in their faith or witnessed for their Lord. It seemed they didn't care! Its committees worked well but without drive. The congregation was revving the motor but had not engaged the gears. It was not as though the church had never been warned. In the letter to Timothy one reads a prophetic voice describing a timid people who are contented with a tepid faith. It had a godly form but lacked the Holy Spirit's power.

But mark this: There will be terrible times in the last days. People will be lovers of themselves, lovers of money, boastful, proud, abusive, disobedient to their parents, ungrateful, unholy, without love, unforgiving, slanderous, without self-control, brutal, not lovers of the good, treacherous, rash, conceited, lovers of pleasure rather than lovers of God — having a form of godliness but denying its power. Have nothing to do with such people (1 Timothy 3:1–5).

Can Sardis be redeemed? It can happen only if the church heeds what the Spirit is saying! The church needs to overcome its acceptance of spiritual mediocrity. God keeps records of those deserving eternal life. The Psalmist (6:28), in resenting his tormenters, asks God to wipe out those who beset him. *"May they be blotted out of the book of life and not be listed with the righteous."* God keeps a register of those who love, obey and serve him faithfully.

Consider the exchange the LORD had with Moses, referring to Moses' Israelite charges succumbing to worship a golden calf: *"Moses went back to the Lord and said, 'Oh, what a great sin these people have committed! They have made themselves gods of gold. But now, please forgive their sin—but if not, then blot me out of the book you have written.' The Lord replied to Moses, 'Whoever has sinned against me I will blot out of my book'"* (Exodus 32:31–34).

To miss being in God's eternal register is damning.

CHAPTER SEVEN

PHILADELPHIA

*"To the angel of the church in Philadelphia write:
These are the words of him who is holy and true,
who holds the key of David. What he opens no one
can shut, and what he shuts no one can open. I know
your deeds. See, I have placed before you an open
door that no one can shut. I know that you have little
strength, yet you have kept my word and have not
denied my name. I will make those who are of the
synagogue of Satan, who claim to be Jews though
they are not, but are liars—I will make them come
and fall down at your feet and acknowledge that I
have loved you. Since you have kept my command to
endure patiently, I will also keep you from the hour
of trial that is going to come on the whole world to
test those who live on the earth.*

*I am coming soon. Hold on to what you have, so that
no one will take your crown. Those who are
victorious I will make pillars in the temple of my
God. Never again will they leave it. I will write on
them the name of my God and the name of the city of
my God, the new Jerusalem, which is coming down*

out of heaven from my God; and I will also write on
them my new name.
Whoever has ears, let them hear what the Spirit says
to the churches" (Revelation 3:7–13).

Some people know a great gift when they see it. They also realize they have been put in a place or situation where opportunity is obvious to them. These people understand that God has placed them where they are to do something special for him. Events and people sometimes come together in a nexus moment. When Queen Esther realized that her Jewish people could suffer a holocaust simply because they were Jews, her uncle Mordecai helped her recognize that opportunity to save them. *"Who knows,"* he said to her, *"that you have come to royal position for such a time as this"* (Esther 4:14b). Opportunity knocks!

At this point in history the church at Philadelphia was in a nexus moment. The church was at a crossroads of history. It was like a sea turtle laying its eggs at the ripe moment, so that when their shells broke, the hatchlings could emerge from the sand, catch the high tide and enter the sea. In one of Shakespeare's plays, Brutus attempts to rationalize his plot to kill the Roman emperor and offers his perspective on his timing.

"There is a tide in the affairs of men,
which, taken at the flood, leads on to fortune;
omitted, all the voyage of their life
is bound in shallows and in miseries.
On such a full sea are we now afloat,
And we must take the current when it serves,

or lose our ventures" (Julius Caesar Act 4, scene 3, 218–224).

Eumenes II of Pergamum founded Philadelphia soon after he ascended Pergamum's throne in 197 BC. King Eumenes named the new city "Philadelphia" in honour of his brother and successor Attalus II. Attalus II was otherwise known as Philadelphus. The name of the city means "city of brotherly love," a title showing Eumenes' deep affection for Attalus.

A major event occurred in Philadelphia in AD 17. Tiberius was newly on the Roman throne. Jesus had finished his apprenticeship as a carpenter under his earthly father Joseph. An earthquake of significance shattered buildings throughout Lydia and Mysia. The city Philadelphia (now known in Turkey as Alaşehir) was smack in the centre of the fault zone. Tiberius had some compassion on the city and excused its citizens from taxation – for a while. In return, the city's citizens enhanced the role of the imperial cult and later built a temple for their Caesar. The appreciative Philadelphians temporarily renamed their city as Neocaesarea.

The poverty of Philadelphia must have been well known throughout Asia Minor. Earthquakes can be shattering in more ways than one. Although it sat on a foremost trade zone, Philadelphia probably suffered severely from that catastrophe. One only needs to consider what happened in Haiti's 2010 earthquake to know that people were squashed, families destroyed, limbs crushed and amputated, while broken bodies were trapped and left to die. Mayhem was everywhere. Ditto in Japan in 2011.

Philadelphia had no earthmovers, cranes, bobcats or tractors to easily remove the broken buildings and houses. People's homes were reduced to rubble and their possessions lost along with their family members. Recovery for the survivors would have taken decades.

A Door of Hope

The prophet Hosea had a positive word for his people amid their suffering. *"Therefore I am now going . . . speak tenderly to her. There I will give her back her vineyards, and will make the Valley of Achor a door of hope [peta tikvah]. There she will respond as in the days of her youth"* (Hosea 2: 14, 15).

The valley bounded by Mysia, Lydia and Phrygia, now torn apart by the region's earthquake, also needed a door of hope. The believers in Philadelphia found a door of hope in their victory over sin and death that Jesus provides for his people. One meaning of the door in this passage relates to hope. *I have placed before you an open door that no one can shut.* Yet there is much more to that open door than just hope, as will be discussed under a following section, "special words."

Philadelphia was on a frontier as well as on a significant commercial trading route. When Alexander the Great galloped through this area almost two centuries earlier, his ambition was to spread the Hellenistic gospel to tribes he conquered. This was followed by the stroke of Antiochus Epiphanes whose ambition likewise was to destroy all civilizations that blocked the "Greek Way." So he too promoted the Hellenization of all the lands, and pushed boundaries into barbarian territory.

Attalus II similarly promoted Greek ideas and culture. That worked until his successor and nephew Attalus III died heirless and endowed his kingdom to Rome. So, Philadelphia was created, in part, to promote everything Greek. Its founding was mission-motivated. It had so many temples it earned the reputation of "little Athens." Philadelphia already served as a door to the future before Jesus' followers took up his cross and exampled their Christian life in that small but significant community.

Religious Profusion

Philadelphia hosted all the regular religions. A robust Jewish presence in the city feasted on the conflux of trade routes allowing them to do business that was kosher. Thus, a strong synagogue existed. The Christian presence was unified and without the heretical versions of Gnosticism or Marcionism that plagued many congregations in the fledgling faith flocks of Asia Minor. Colossae may have had a cozy clique committed to worship angels within its church membership but Philadelphia was free from that or other digressions. The city, including the little band of believers, may have been dirt poor but the church was rich with faith.

Christians in Philadelphia took the content of 1 Timothy 6:17–19 seriously:

Command those who are rich in this present world not to be arrogant nor to put their hope in wealth, which is so uncertain, but to put their hope in God, who richly provides us with everything for our enjoyment. Command them to do good, to be rich in good deeds, and to be generous and willing to share.

In this way they will lay up treasure for themselves
as a firm foundation for the coming age, so that they
may take hold of the life that is truly life.

Among the pagan religions all the usual suspects
were established in the city, especially since the municipality
was intended by its founders to be a staging ground for
Greek culture. Likely the temples were much less ornate
than their Ephesus or Pergamum counterparts. All
communities required physicians, so the popular priests of
Asklepios were present and likely a token temple existed for
their adoration. The larger healing centres of Kos (near
Patmos) and Epidauros on the Peloponnese mainland had
elaborate temples to Asklepios. They also became training
venues. There, doctor-priests like Hippocrates could expand
their medical knowledge and then share it.

The imperial cult existed with its temple to the
divine Caesar. Fertility cults abounded and practised their
zealous rites in modest temples dedicated to Zeus, Artemis,
Aphrodite, Apollo, Cybele, Magna Mater, Demeter (Ceres,
in Rome), Dionysus, Hestia, Pan, Athena, Nike, Ares and
representative sanctuaries of some mystery religions. Some
of the older pagan deities before Hellenistic culture
developed also surfaced in Philadelphia, such as Ba'al and
Mot, once a part of the passé Syrian pantheon.

In truth, the poor and picayune Philadelphia began
as a buffer zone. Like Thyatira, it served to protect
Pergamum. Its purpose was to be a "canary in the coal
mine," despite the half fiction of a brother's love. The tender
naming by Eumenes II after his brother is more romantic
thought than veracity. It is a good cover story. The city had
something of an inferiority complex, possibly because

Philadelphians knew its true purpose. In addition to being a staging point for Hellenism into the barbarian world, Philadelphia was also a siren and sacrifice in case any armed forces threatened Pergamum. In a way, Philadelphians were bit actors in the larger drama of life issues in Pergamum and Smyrna.

Not so the minor church pulsating in earthquake-prone Philadelphia! It held a major responsible task assigned to its members by Jesus himself. The humble Christian community perched on the fertile volcanic plain to its east, was commissioned by its Lord to germinate faith in the people venturing on the trading routes passing through its community.

Caravans passed by here with timetable regularity. Travelling merchants came from every compass point on their way to every other compass point. Like those visiting Jerusalem at Pentecost, folks from every nation and of every tongue heard the story of Jesus, his death and resurrection. In Jerusalem, three thousand of them responded in one day to accept God's gift of salvation. It could happen in Philadelphia – and it did. The people of that city took every opportunity to share their rich faith with peripatetic agents.

Some of these merchants were Jews who networked with the sizable Jewish population of Philadelphia. The entrenched synagogue supervisors belittled the Christians who spoke about Messiah Jesus. The bad spirit resulted in an unhappy tension of Jews and believers in Philadelphia as we note in 3:9.

This passage is not an anti-Semitic sentiment but a

statement of fact that some of the Jews, likely the synagogue authorities, were dogging the church by bullying and harassing them. In the gospels, particularly the Fourth Gospel, the evangelist often uses the phrase "the Jews" when he means a portion of the Sanhedrin, and not the general Jewish population. For example, the NIV corrects the misrepresentation in the KJV where "fear of the Jews" provides the wrong message. NIV translates the intent of John 19:38 as, *"Joseph of Arimathea asked Pilate for the body of Jesus. Now Joseph was a disciple of Jesus, but secretly because he feared the Jewish leaders."*

Special Words

This section devoted to apprize Philadelphia of their ministry of the Lord's commission to them contains some coded words. They are: "open door," "holy one," "key of David," "synagogue of Satan," "bow down," "those who dwell on the earth," "temple pillar," and special names.

The "open door" was the opening God placed before the church to evangelize people passing through their municipality or stopping at their several inns and caravansaries. Opportunity surrounded this church. Jesus once had said to his disciples:

> *I tell you, open your eyes and look at the fields! They are ripe for harvest. Even now those who reap draw their wages, even now they harvest the crop for eternal life, so that the sower and the reaper may be glad together. Thus the saying, 'One sows and another reaps' is true. I sent you to reap what you have not worked for. Others have done the hard work, and you have reaped the benefits of their labour* (John 4:35b–38).

Some churches overlook every prospect God offers them. When a visitor attends a worship service, for example, the ushers or leaders miss out if they do not get the visitors' names or their addresses. God sends visitors to the churches that have a mission mentality. Mission churches care about people, their needs and their talents. They know that newcomers are insecure in their new community or are enduring a situation in which they need a loving ear. Philadelphia had members who cared about people in their neighbourhood and even in traversing their travel lanes.

The text refers to "the holy one, the true one." The reference, of course, is to Jesus. He is not like the false deities venerated in Philadelphia. *"We know also that the Son of God has come and has given us understanding, so that we may know him who is true. And we are in him who is true by being in his Son Jesus Christ. He is the true God and eternal life"* (1 John 5:20). Jesus' words are those of a king whose edicts cannot be questioned. He is holy, and therefore his words are sacred, hallowed and must be respected.

"The Holy One of Israel" is a phrase frequently used in the Old Testament to reverence God. His name is so sacred it cannot be written. The expression is a euphemism, so that the writer and reader will not blaspheme God's name. Isaiah, for example wrote (20:14–15): *"This is what the Lord says—your Redeemer, the Holy One of Israel: "For your sake I will send to Babylon and bring down as fugitives all the Babylonians, in the ships in which they took pride. I am the Lord, your Holy One, Israel's Creator, your King"* (and so on). Philadelphians reading this scroll brought to them by Prochorus needed confirmation that the text was authentic.

The phrase "Key of David" probably riled the leaders in the synagogue of Satan. It is a symbol of trust. Hezekiah, king of Judah, entrusted his treasury to Eliakim, a servant. Eliakim controlled all access to the king's palace. He acted as appointment secretary to the king. A reference is in Isaiah's prophecy (22:20–26):

> *"In that day I will summon my servant, Eliakim son of Hilkiah. I will clothe him with your robe and fasten your sash around him and hand your authority over to him. He will be a father to those who live in Jerusalem and to the house of Judah. I will place on his shoulder the key to the house of David; what he opens no one can shut, and what he shuts no one can open. I will drive him like a peg into a firm place; he will become a seat of honour for the house of his father."*

In a word, Jesus "trusted" his church to serve him and spread his gospel. This commendation to the Christians in the city was also a condemnation to the local synagogue rulers who were not inclusive in their sharing God's mercy, love and salvation to others. Clearly, to Jesus, Satan was now ruling the synagogue and not God. Jesus, not Satan, controlled the opportunities afforded his followers.

The synagogue of Satan is Jesus' disapproval of the Jewish leadership in the city. These Jews made trouble for Christians in an assortment of obstructions. They may have bad-mouthed those who spoke of Jesus as Messiah, boycotted their market goods, withheld loans or falsely witnessed their character. Jesus is countering the assumption of the Jews that God loves them more than others. This group in Philadelphia's synagogue simply did not believe what God told them through Isaiah and Ezekiel.

For this is what the Lord says: "To the eunuchs who keep my Sabbaths, who choose what pleases me and hold fast to my covenant—to them I will give within my temple and its walls a memorial and a name better than sons and daughters; I will give them an everlasting name that will endure forever. And foreigners who bind themselves to the Lord to minister to him, to love the name of the Lord, and to be his servants, all who keep the Sabbath without desecrating it and who hold fast to my covenant— these I will bring to my holy mountain and give them joy in my house of prayer. Their burnt offerings and sacrifices will be accepted on my altar; for my house will be called a house of prayer for all nations" (Isaiah 56:4–6).

"Therefore say to the house of Israel, 'This is what the Sovereign Lord says: It is not for your sake, house of Israel, that I am going to do these things, but for the sake of my holy name, which you have profaned among the nations where you have gone. I will show the holiness of my great name, which has been profaned among the nations, the name you have profaned among them. Then the nations will know that I am the Lord, declares the Sovereign Lord, when I am proved holy through you before their eyes" (Ezekiel 36:22, 23).

For this reason, the instruction of Jesus is that the Jews will bow down to Jesus. Israel is no longer the primacy. The new Israel, as Paul indicated to the Romans, is the Church of Jesus Christ. *"It is not as though God's word had failed. For not all who are descended from Israel are Israel. Nor because they are his descendants are they all Abraham's children"* (Romans 9:6, 7).

Tragically, the Jews were too earthly-minded to

receive God's praise. "Those who dwell on the earth" were not conscious of the spiritual level that was requisite to understand God's truth.

God rewards faithfulness. Jesus says that the Christians of Philadelphia are "pillars in the temple" of God. Peter used a similar metaphor to describe God's people. *"As you come to him, the living Stone—rejected by human beings but chosen by God and precious to him—you also, like living stones, are being built into a spiritual house to be a holy priesthood, offering spiritual sacrifices acceptable to God through Jesus Christ"* (1 Peter 2:4, 5).

Last of all, we have repetition of the term "name." *"You have kept my word and have not denied my name"* (v. 8). As mentioned previously, name represented the person. "Name" meant character, honour, and essence. *"I will write on him the name of my God,"* means that believers in this city belong to God, and belong to him because they have been true and loyal to him *"The name of the city of my God"* means that Philadelphians have dual citizenship. They live in that city but they also inhabit and inherit the commonwealth of God. They will inherit the new Jerusalem God is creating for them. *"My own new name,"* is the designation that Jesus is exalted and sovereign over all history and known only to those who have his Spirit dwelling within them. Jesus' use of *"My God,"* suggests the impregnable, inseparable link of Jesus' true followers with God himself.

Philadelphia's Report Card

Philadelphians need never be ashamed of their report card. God is proud of them. He gladly allows them to be associated with him. He will never deny them; they have never denied him. They are loyal, dependable, strong in faith, unbending under harassment and inflexible when false witness confronts them.

They had no need to feel inadequate simply because they were poor. God has given them a laurel crown of victory (they earned their laurels!). In God's eyes, they were giants of a winning faith and an attractive love.

CHAPTER EIGHT

LAODICEA

"To the angel of the church in Laodicea write:

These are the words of the Amen, the faithful and true witness, the ruler of God's creation. I know your deeds, that you are neither cold nor hot. I wish you were either one or the other! So, because you are lukewarm—neither hot nor cold—I am about to spit you out of my mouth. You say, 'I am rich; I have acquired wealth and do not need a thing.' But you do not realize that you are wretched, pitiful, poor, blind and naked. I counsel you to buy from me gold refined in the fire, so you can become rich; and white clothes to wear, so you can cover your shameful nakedness; and salve to put on your eyes, so you can see.

Those whom I love I rebuke and discipline. So be earnest, and repent. Here I am! I stand at the door and knock. If anyone hears my voice and opens the door, I will come in and eat with them, and they with me.

To those who are victorious, I will give the right to

sit with me on my throne, just as I was victorious and sat down with my Father on his throne. Whoever has ears, let them hear what the Spirit says to the churches" (Revelation 3:14–22).

Having delivered this praiseworthy message to Philadelphia, Prochorus moved on to his last destination to deliver his seventh and final scroll. The seventh pastoral visit was to Laodicea, about 70 kilometers southeast of Philadelphia.

The city was cradled below the snow-covered hills to the south and the plateau 10 kilometers to the north on which Hierapolis stood. Laodicea was elevated on its own lesser plateau above the Lycus River plain separating it from Hierapolis. Recent excavations have begun to expose the streets and buildings of biblical Laodicea.

Laodicea was part of a tri-city, with Hierapolis on the north and Colossae on the east. Epaphras (Epaphroditus) is the one who likely evangelized the area. Paul sent messages to Colossae through him. Philip is said to have brought the gospel to Hierapolis. The church named a basilica there after him. Part of its ruins still denote its Hierapolitan location.

Perhaps Epaphras brought the "Good News" to Laodicea as well. Hierapolis sported several thermal springs and became a healing centre. Hierapolis hosted athletic contests and dramas and saw famous people rewarded for their deeds. Colossae's congregation had some quirky members who strayed from normative Christian faith to endorse the worship of angels. Paul gently, yet sharply, rebuked the Colossian church for that excess (Colossians 2:4–8).

Laodicea's name derived from the wife of Antiochus II – Laodikea. The date of its founding seems to be about 250 BC, but it may have sprung from villages already in existence at that time. Perhaps Epahras went through the area telling the gospel message. Believers gathered and organized themselves from Epaphras' evangelism and consequently formed a church. Like Sardis and Philadelphia, the city suffered from the same earthquake system that had leveled the cities numbered five and six on the "circle of seven churches."

Spirituality in the City

Spiritually, Laodicea was a mixture of pagan religion emphasizing fertility, and Greek mythology to honour Zeus and his Mount Olympus tribe. Blended in with the Greek emphases were Phrygian deities often wearing the mask for their Greek equivalents. Asklepios became Men Karou in this scenario. A major temple to Men Karou existed within a few kilometers of the city and its priests carried out the tradition of medicine also associated with Asklepios. Theirs was a specialized medicine, ophthalmology. Add in the imperial cult, drawing on its own admirers and supporters. Jewish traders in their Diaspora found a toehold in Laodicea. And then there was this church, the seventh church in the traveling round that Prochorus visited.

Jesus did not think much of the charitable acts of people in this church. Their works, said Jesus, were neither hot nor cold. Their works were not out of charity but in pursuit of the proverbial cash register (or its Hellenistic equivalent). The Christian people were financially ambitious.

The reference to "hot and cold" is to the water from thermal streams eastward along the Lycus Valley and the melting snow water falling from the high hills to the south. Pipes, still evident, show how the water was channeled into Laodicea. They reveal how the cold water was no longer cold and the hot water no longer hot by the time it reached the city. Moreover, the sulphur in the water gave it a most disagreeable taste. Jesus said, "*I am about to spew it out of my mouth.*"

They were an industrious people, these Laodiceans, and the church in the city prospered from it. Did their guilds with their pagan deities compromise the believers in that city? We do not know. Industry has its own way of setting community standards and sometimes the standards conflict horribly with Christian morality and ethics. No sign is evident that Christians made much fuss about such things as principles.

The Money Merchants

Banking was a major industry in the city. The "bean counter" accountants watched their chattels carefully. They knew debits from assets. Laodicea was yacht rich. Jesus warned his disciples about loving money or being too involved with things that took away from love, mercy and justice. He bade his followers not to look at bank ledgers when they sought to help people. *"Let your light shine before men,"* he said, *"that they may see your good works and praise your Father in Heaven"* (Matthew 5:16). *"When you give to the poor,"* he noted, (using the left ledger as the debit side and the right ledger as the asset side) *"do not let your left hand know what your right hand is doing"* (Matthew 6:3). Jesus was saying that acts of love are not determined by a budget. The Timothy letters underscored this principle. *"For the love of money is a root of all kinds of evil. Some people, eager for money, have wandered from the faith and pierced themselves with many griefs"* (1 Timothy 6:10).

These bankers learned their craft from Sardis' gold standards. Their city was the Fort Knox of the Phrygian world. When Sardis and Philadelphia took handouts from Tiberius to rebuild their infrastructures, Laodicean bankers refused all Roman capital advances. "We will rebuild our own city, thank you, Tiberius! We'll do it ourselves!" And with good reason! Tiberius could not own them. Pride was the motive here, however, not liberty.

This attitude brushed off on the church. Christians seemed to want God at a distance where the church would not be obligated to him. Had they forgotten that they were beholden to him? Who died for their sins? Who had offered them and provided them with eternal life? Had they forgotten the source of grace? It seems that the Laodicean church had shunted God to a spur line.

Shepherds and Their Wool

Shepherds in and around Laodicea were wise to genetic breeding. Like Jacob [see Genesis 30:31 *ff.*] they may not have known about chromosomes and genes but they knew selective propagation. These sheep exhibited very dark wool. Weavers developed the glossy black wool into sheets, clothing and carpets. In turn, along with the wool yarn, clothiers hawked their wares throughout the empires of Alexander the Great, the Antiochus family, the Ptolemy tribes and the Romans. A woolen tunic developed from the yarn, called the Trimitaria. It became a "must have" item for global fashion status seekers. Merchants around the world could not get enough of these tunics. The coats were constantly in demand by shopkeepers. Those clothing reps who wholesaled the Trimitaria became wealthy from their unique product. The Trimitaria was the "Rolex watch" of Asian clothing.

Laodicea's School of Medicine

Laodicea was likewise famous for, and rich because of, its ophthalmological centre. This centre was a temple west of the city toward Carura that venerated the Phrygian god Men Karou. The myth of this lunar Phrygian deity Men was almost identical to the Greek myth of Asklepios. Phrygian deities tended to connect with phases of the moon. Men's identity was a crescent moon. Men, in this lunar form of Olympus, was responsible to safeguard the crops, visit the underworld and protect tombs of the dead. Phrygians also associated Men with healing.

The medical priests at Karou had developed a salve and, in pill and powder form, a tablet for treating eye troubles. When exported, the tablet could be ground to power and with a water solution, mid-eastern pharmacists would apply the lotion to the affected eyes. The Mediterranean world experienced considerable blindness, or situations leading to blindness. Dust was prevalent in the mid-eastern air. It led to conjunctivitis, or red eye. The "Phrygian powder," as it was called, seemed to heal conjunctivitis, and perhaps, by using the solution, slow down the development of cataracts.

Cataracts result from several other causes, of course. Trachoma and Glaucoma added to eye issues. Injury from war (military ophthalmia) and work hazards might lead to cataracts. Shortages of Vitamin A and other chemicals, plus infection by certain flies that cause "river blindness' (onchoceriasis) are contributors. Leprosy, diabetes and poor hygienic habits sponsor blindness. One surgeon (Susruta) in India, living at the time of King David, had some insight into the disorder and succeeded in removing cataracts even with relatively crude instruments (see Theodore Berland and Richard A. Perrit, *Living with Your Eye Operation*, p. 80).

Blindness was a major social issue. Many without vision were forced to beg for food. Many blind people bumped into things and injured themselves. Some fell, broke limbs or died. No wonder the Mediterranean world liked Laodicea. Pilgrims trooped there for treatment. Exporters of

Phrygian powder watched their affluence increase. Laodicea had done well in the health market.

The Laodicean Church's Report Card

Laodicea had not done well in God's ledger, however. On a scale of one to seven, this church was close to zero. This dog had serious fleas and did not know it. It sported a shallow but smug spirituality. Laodicea's church light was hidden under a thick basket, its salt lacked its preservative quality. The people "enjoyed" a surfeit of the world's goods. The city took too much pride in its DIY (do it yourself) attitude. "We're all right Jack," was their response to everybody and everything.

Caring About Our Neighbours and Neighbourhoods

If Philadelphia got an A-Plus for its gospel ministry, Laodicea earned an F-Minus. The seventh church was a complete contrast to the sixth. Philadelphia was humble. Laodicea was proud. Philadelphia was sharing and outgoing. Laodicea was smug and self-satisfied. Philadelphia was Christ-centred. Laodicea kept Christ out of its affairs. Philadelphia modeled the missionary motif. Laodicea cared little about those outside its cozy club life. Jesus said, "I know your works!" What works? Laodicea's causes were all commercial and crass. They reflected nothing but a monetary bottom line. Jesus knew that! Where was love? Where was mercy? Where was mission? Where was compassion?

By the time *Revelation* was in scroll form, the Four Gospels were written and in full circulation. The complete New Testament was not yet standardized but Jesus' words, his acts of healing, his authentic instructions and the ample accounts of his passion – suffering, death, resurrection and ascension were well known by every believer. Moreover, Paul's letters had been widely circulated and were *de rigueur* reading in all churches.

The essence of the Christian faith is "faith." As Paul indicated in several letters (Galatians 3:6–9) (Ephesians 2:4–10) (Romans 10:9–11), faith and trust of a believer in Jesus' work on the cross was what counted with God. Even then, it was God who gave them the grace to have faith. "Doing" did not work when it came to salvation.

When a clever man approached Jesus about salvation, he asked Jesus what he must "do" to inherit eternal life. What Jesus wanted him to "do" was to "believe." If he believed in Jesus he would give his possessions to the needy of society and then follow Jesus as his disciple, would he not? What must I *do*? (see John 10:28; Mark 10:17; Luke 10:25 18:18; 1 John 5: 13).

When Paul ministered to the Philippian jailer who had beaten, then had imprisoned the apostle and his companion, the prison keeper asked about salvation. Paul and Silas answered his apprehensive query, *"Sirs, what must I do to be saved?"* They replied, *"Believe in the Lord Jesus, and you will be saved"* (Acts 16:30, 31).

Faith in Jesus as Saviour and Lord, however is one-dimensional. It is a vertical relationship. Faith in Jesus also requires a horizontal relationship with others. James pointed his Jerusalem believers to the biblical truth of the "royal law." *"If you really keep the royal law found in Scripture* [Lev. 19:8], *'Love your neighbor as yourself,' you are doing right"* (James 2:8). And as James further wrote,

> *What good is it, my brothers and sisters, if people claim to have faith but have no deeds? Can such faith save them? Suppose a brother or sister is without clothes and daily food. If one of you says to them, "Go in peace; keep warm and well fed," but does nothing about their physical needs, what good is it? In the same way, faith by itself, if it is not accompanied by action, is dead. But someone will say, "You have faith; I have deeds."*

> *Show me your faith without deeds, and I will show you my faith by what I do. You believe that there is one God. Good! Even the demons believe that—and shudder. You foolish person, do you want evidence that faith without deeds is useless?* (James 2:14–20).

Jesus' own words speak harshly to Laodicea"

> *"Then he will say to those on his left, 'Depart from me, you who are cursed, into the eternal fire prepared for the devil and his angels. For I was hungry and you gave me nothing to eat, I was thirsty and you gave me nothing to drink, I was a stranger and you did not invite me in, I needed clothes and you did not clothe me, I was sick and in prison and you did not look after me.'*

> *"They also will answer, 'Lord, when did we see you hungry or thirsty or a stranger or needing clothes or sick or in prison, and did not help you?' "He will*

130

reply, *'Truly I tell you, whatever you did not do for one of the least of these, you did not do for me.'* *"Then they will go away to eternal punishment, but the righteous to eternal life"* (Matthew 25:41–46).

In *The Acts of the Apostles*, Luke records Peter as noting that Jesus did works of love, healing, encouraging and gently teaching the people of Galilee and Judah.

> *You know the message God sent to the people of Israel, announcing the good news of peace through Jesus Christ, who is Lord of all. You know what has happened throughout the province of Judea, beginning in Galilee after the baptism that John preached—how God anointed Jesus of Nazareth with the Holy Spirit and power, and how he went around doing good and healing all who were under the power of the devil, because God was with him* (Acts 10:36–38).

In his teaching letter to the Philippian believers, the Apostle Paul made a point of illustrating servanthood as modeled by Jesus.

> *In your relationships with one another, have the same attitude of mind Christ Jesus had: Who, being in very nature God, did not consider equality with God something to be used to his own advantage; rather, he made himself nothing by taking the very nature of a servant, being made in human likeness.*
> *And being found in appearance as a human being, he humbled himself by becoming obedient to death — even death on a cross! Therefore God exalted him to the highest place and gave him the name that is above every name, that at the name of Jesus every knee should bow, in heaven and on earth and under*

the earth, and every tongue acknowledge that Jesus Christ is Lord, to the glory of God the Father (Philippians 2:1–11).

One cannot read what Jesus said without understanding the horizontal line with other humans that must accompany the vertical line of a divine relationship.

"The kings of the Gentiles lord it over them; and those who exercise authority over them call themselves Benefactors. But you are not to be like that. Instead, the greatest among you should be like the youngest, and the one who rules like the one who serves. For who is greater, the one who is at the table or the one who serves? Is it not the one who is at the table? But I am among you as one who serves (Luke 22:25–27).

The believers in Laodicea allowed this teaching to waft over their heads. They didn't get it. Consequently, we have stressed this rejoinder from Jesus in this chapter. Christ's Church must be as earthly-minded as it is heavenly-minded. It cannot be a holy huddle, a cozy clique or a closed club. The church does not exist for itself. It is an agent of God's love in the world. God's love is best illustrated by Jesus who gave himself both to his heavenly Father and to others without strings attached to his love.

Wretched, Poor, Naked and Blind

Jesus instructed, not just invited, the Laodicean Christians to look directly into God's unblemished mirror. They must see themselves as God sees them. They have forgotten who they are and whose they are. James has a word for this church too.

> *Those who listen to the word but do not do what it says are like people who look at their faces in a mirror and, after looking at themselves, go away and immediately forget what they look like. But those who look intently into the perfect law that gives freedom, and continue in it—not forgetting what they have heard, but doing it—they will be blessed in what they do* (James 1:23–25).

Building on what the Laodiceans do in their community – dealing in banks and gold, specializing in black *haut couture* garments and salving eyes red from conjunctivitis – Jesus tells them the truth they avoid.

Their bank vaults protected their refined gold possession. But their gold was improperly refined. It was more like dross. Their tunics were globally-acclaimed and their restoration of vision to the sightless was renowned. But they were wearing the wrong coloured clothing. They thought of themselves as dapper dressers. But they were naked. They produced medicines to cure conjunctivitis but they were totally sightless about their own sin.

> *You say, 'I am rich; I have acquired wealth and do not need a thing.' But you do not realize that you are wretched, pitiful, poor, blind and naked. I counsel you to buy from me gold refined in the fire, so you can become rich; and white clothes to wear, so you can cover your shameful nakedness; and salve to put on your eyes, so you can see* (Revelation 3:17, 18).

Required Repentance

Jesus is brutally frank in his report card to this Church. The Church was not yet rejected by God. Yet it needed immediate changing. Repentance for its failures was in order. Repentance (*metanoia*) is doing a complete U-turn in one's thinking and in one's behaviour. The word translated *earnest* can also be translated *zealous*. The command then, is "be earnest in your repentance" (mean what you say and do) and/or *"be zealous in your repentance"* (repent with conviction). God does not want a tepid or token repentance.

Jesus is not happy about what he sees in this church. But he does not write it off. *"Those whom I love I rebuke and discipline."* This is a statement of hope for any church off the rails. God does not give up on us. He leaves room for us to turn around. U-turns are permitted on the highway to hell. God offers second chances.

Jesus told the Laodiceans, "Allow Christ inside your lives and my church. Find my fellowship." In his letter to Colossae, Paul asks that the churches at Hierapolis and Laodicea be alerted to his love. Likely the Colossian epistle also went to them. If so, Paul's words fully reflected those of Jesus to this Seventh Church. *So then, just as you received Christ Jesus as Lord, continue to live your lives in him, rooted and built up in him, strengthened in the faith as you were taught, and overflowing with thankfulness* (Colossians 2:6, 7).

In his letter to Corinthian believers, Paul advised

them of his ambitions to be as close to God as possible. He wanted to live like that all the time, no matter what. Dwight L. Moody is reported as saying, "Character is what a man is in the dark." Paul stated, *We make it our goal to please him, whether we are at home in the body or away from it. For we must all appear before the judgment seat of Christ, that everyone may receive what is due them for the things done while in the body, whether good or bad* (2 Corinthians 5:9, 10).

Finding fellowship with God was what the Jews understood as *halakah*. When Isaiah wrote, "*they shall walk and not faint*" (Isaiah 40:11) he was referring to keeping a godly walk. That is *halakah*. *Halakah* is thriving on God's presence, delighting in his commands and poring over his instructions, so as to walk in unison with him. Psalm 119 suggests such an intention: "*Blessed are those whose ways are blameless, who walk according to the law of the Lord. Blessed are those who keep his statutes and seek him with all their heart—they do no wrong but follow his ways*" (119:1–3).

Paul understood *halakah* as being "*in Christ.*" He used this phrase many times to write about a rich and unshakeable fellowship with the Lord Jesus Christ. "*Therefore, if anyone is in Christ, the new creation has come: The old has gone, the new is here!*" (2 Corinthians 5:17).

Jesus described *halakah* with a different metaphor. It is precisely what the Church at Laodicea needed to hear. Jesus wanted this brand of fellowship with his church and he wanted his church to have all the privileges and joy that went with his fellowship.

> *Remain in me, as I also remain in you. No branch can bear fruit by itself; it must remain in the vine. Neither can you bear fruit unless you remain in me. "I am the vine; you are the branches. If you remain in me and I in you, you will bear much fruit; apart from me you can do nothing. If you do not remain in me, you are like a branch that is thrown away and withers; such branches are picked up, thrown into the fire and burned. If you remain in me and my words remain in you, ask whatever you wish, and it will be done for you. This is to my Father's glory, that you bear much fruit, showing yourselves to be my disciples* (John 15:4–8).

Those ears again!

Churches as well as individuals in them need a constant awareness of God's presence with them. God walks with his people every day and every way. He constantly gives alerts, encouragements, instructions and corrections so that believers separately and together will understand his will for them. Isaiah's prophetic voice will ring true when we listen. *"Then the eyes of those who see will no longer be closed, and the ears of those who hear will listen"* (Isaiah 32:3).

> *Hear, you deaf; look, you blind, and see! Who is blind but my servant, and deaf like the messenger I send? Who is blind like the one in covenant with me, blind like the servant of the Lord? You have seen many things, but have paid no attention; your ears are open, but you hear nothing"* (Isaiah 42:18–20).

The message comes often enough that churches can hardly miss it. Perhaps they have stopped listening. Laodicea had. The septet of Asia Minor churches were each and all strongly instructed to "listen up." The Lord of the church spoke on this matter also. *"Do you still not see or understand? Are your hearts hardened? Do you have eyes but fail to see, and ears but fail to hear? And don't you remember?"* (Mark 8:18). Consider history stuttering with the same messages . . .

> *Your eyes have seen all that the Lord did in Egypt to Pharaoh, to all his officials and to all his land. With your own eyes you saw those great trials, those signs and great wonders. But to this day the Lord has not given you a mind that understands or eyes that see or ears that hear* (Deuteronomy 29:2–4).

> *Son of man, you are living among a rebellious people. They have eyes to see but do not see and ears to hear but do not hear, for they are a rebellious people* (Ezekiel 12:2).

> *When he said this, he called out, "Whoever has ears to hear, let them hear." His disciples asked him what this parable meant. He said, "The knowledge of the secrets of the kingdom of God has been given to you, but to others I speak in parables, so that, 'though seeing, they may not see; though hearing, they may not understand.' "This is the meaning of the parable: The seed is the word of God. Those along the path are the ones who hear, and then the devil comes and takes away the word from their hearts, so that they may not believe and be saved. Those on the rock are the ones who receive the word with joy when they hear it, but they have no root. They believe for a while, but in the time of testing they fall away. The seed that fell among thorns stands for*

137

those who hear, but as they go on their way they are
choked by life's worries, riches and pleasures, and
they do not mature. But the seed on good soil stands
for those with a noble and good heart, who hear the
word, retain it, and by persevering produce a crop
(Luke 8:8–15).

Salt is good, but if it loses its saltiness, how can it be
made salty again? It is fit neither for the soil nor for
the manure pile; it is thrown out. Whoever has ears
to hear, let them hear (Luke 14:34, 35).

In the first three chapters of *The Revelation of Jesus Christ* has repeated what needed continual stressing. Those who manage to turn their lives over to God, Jesus will welcome back. As he voiced his willing redemption, he invited the Laodicean church in particular to note from where he gives his invitation. *To those who are victorious, I will give the right to sit with me on my throne, just as I was victorious and sat down with my Father on his throne. Whoever has ears, let them hear what the Spirit says to the churches"* (Revelation 3:14–22).

He is on a throne. It is the throne of David, from whose human line he was begotten. He sits also on the throne given him by his Father. It is a throne of victory over death and sin. It is a resurrection throne. It is a throne most glorious, holy and righteous. He calls, knocks at the Church's door and asks to be invited in – to forgive and fellowship with his family. But what if the church family refuses to hear him rapping on the door? Pray they are not that wanting.

138

CHAPTER NINE

EPILOGUE

... And Personal Observations

Some tag ends remain from this book's eight preceding chapters. The third chapter ends with Jesus asking the "Seventh Church" to invite him into its "inner sanctum." Table fellowship was exceedingly important to those in a Mid-eastern culture. To keep Jesus outside was unthinkable. The 23rd Psalm reminds everyone how crucial was hosting for such societies. *"You prepare a table before me in the presence of my enemies."* If a host protects his guest against his enemies, how much more should the Church provide the ambience in which the head of the church may have fellowship with his Church.

The point is that Jesus seeks communion with those who call him Sovereign. This places urgency on those called the Church. Jesus does not want to intrude on our lives. He does want to be in our midst to have the kind of intimacy that transpires when individuals gather around a table for private fellowship and necessary nourishment. Jesus is ready to offer his solutions to a given need. Jesus is ready to reveal his deepest hopes, his great divine knowledge, his abiding power and his concerns and messages for those he loves. So, will the Church as a whole or in part open its door to the Christ who seeks fellowship with his own? That is a crucial question for all the churches in all epochs of history.

Prochorus

We introduced deacon Prochorus early in this book (page 30). It is tradition, not fact, that this deacon toted the seven scrolls and distributed them one at a time to the "Circle of Seven." If not Prochorus, then who? I like that tradition and will stick with that. But I know it is not necessarily fact.

John

Scholars are interested in tracking not only the written word and its origins, but also its authors. In textual preaching, the preacher always needs to know the context of scriptural passages. The well-worn rule is, "a text without the context is a pretext." A homily takes note of (1) what the word says, (2) what the word means and (3) how the word applies.

The author of any writing is likewise important to the credibility of any scripture. This writer takes the view that the author of *Revelation* is that same John whom Jesus called as a disciple while he was mending nets at the shore of Galilee. The proposition has merit. If he had been a very young man when Jesus beckoned him (p. 24), he would be a very old man when *Revelation* was penned. So why not John the disciple as the one who penned *Revelation*?

142

Scholars, rightly, are analysts and skeptics. They like corroborative facts. They compare styles of writing. Sometimes they forget that some authors improve or lose their writing skills over the years. Some scholars, therefore, are prepared to offer alternative authorships. They wonder if John as in *Revelation*, is the same one who wrote the three epistles using John's name. Sometimes scholars refer to John as "John the Theologian" or "John the Divine." (Divine means teacher).

When I studied the Johannine writings "years ago," my seminar professor said, "It was definitely written by John or someone with the same name." His point is correct. The true author is not John but Jesus.

Observations and Applications

Apparently God watches us – close up (see p.14). Bette Midler offered a song in the early 1990s that reminded the world that God is watching us. She sang,

> From a distance. It's the hope of hopes, it's the love of loves. This is the song of every man. And God is watching us, God is watching us, God is watching us from a distance. Oh, God is watching us, God is watching. God is watching us from a distance.

God observes us, watches his church from a distance, of course. He also inspects us up close. He assesses what we do and how well we do it. He intimately knows how we manage the details of our lives and work. He knows when we slack or invest our "all" in what we do. He encourages us to change mediocrity into first class behaviour.

Life is not a rehearsal. *For we will all stand before God's judgment seat. So then, we will all give an account of ourselves to God. Therefore let us stop passing judgment on one another. Instead, make up your mind not to put any stumbling block or obstacle in the way of a brother or sister* (Romans 14:10, 13). We are not judged by our own standards nor by norms others accept, but by the response-ability we have to God alone. Can the Church open its ears to hear that?

Club House Mentality

The Church of Jesus is a fellowship, for sure. But it is not a closed communion. It is neither a clique nor club but an organism. It is not a holy huddle that meets only to call its own plays. The church is far too often forgetful of its purposes. It gathers to worship, study and share its mutual communion. It scatters to act out its assignments and invoke its mission responsibilities. It is always under the command of the Sovereign Jesus. Every committee of every board in every church must answer to the direct instructions of Jesus, Lord of the Church, Head of the Body of Christ. Regrettably, most churches are far too selective in which of Jesus' instructions they obey.

Orally, Please

Read the letters aloud – remember the ears! If it's not read aloud, who can hear it? *"Blessed are those who hear it and take to heart what is written . . ."* (Revelation 1:3). Private reading of God's Word is commendable, even expected, but when a believer group gathers together to worship God it is the Word of God that bonds and teaches them. The Lord intended that the written scroll be read aloud in every Church assembly. *"Blessed is the one who reads aloud this prophecy."* In each of the seven letters, the phrase indicates this command: *"He who has an ear, let him hear what the Spirit says to the churches."* Hear how the Apostle Paul puts it:

> *If the trumpet does not sound a clear call, who will get ready for battle? So it is with you. Unless you speak intelligible words with your tongue, how will anyone know what you are saying? You will just be speaking into the air. Undoubtedly there are all sorts of languages in the world, yet none of them is without meaning. If then I do not grasp the meaning of what someone is saying, I am a foreigner to the speaker, and the speaker is a foreigner to me. So it is with you* (1 Corinthians 14:8–12).

I hope modern churches heed that injunction. Far too many times when I have vacationed in evangelical churches I have not heard God's Word read aloud. The Word is usually in a preacher's sermon, sometimes projected on a video screen to underscore a point in his or her homily. Even then it is secondary to what the preacher is saying in his own words. Liturgical churches do better. Evangelical churches often replace the oral reading of scripture with "worship songs."

Probably the churches axe an oral reading of God's Word because of an artificial time limit imposed by modern congregations obeying the popular TV model. Who dictates time limits to worship? The worship or praise songs may go on for 20–25 minutes but they are no substitute for God's Word being read aloud to a worshipping congregation. God's Word stands by itself. It is its own sermon. It is what God wants his people to hear. The Spirit says, *"Blessed are those*

145

who hear it and take to heart what is written." "Let them hear what the Spirit says . . ."

The Rest of the Story

Paul Harvey always ended his newscasts with a story to solve an incomplete narrative. Then he began to add to it, bringing the listener up to speed. He was a master at hooking the listener, drawing out the article and finishing it off with a twist and his punch line, "And now you know . . . the rest of the story." The first three chapters of this biblical book tell only about the relationship between Jesus and his Church. The remaining 19 chapters of *Revelation* consist of a fascinating twist until the reader comes to the point of learning "the rest of the story."

This book does not cover "the rest of the story." We can give a meagre hint as to what it says. It is about the ferociousness and insidiousness of evil, a foulness so utterly black and rotten that we cannot completely comprehend it. The rest of the story is also that one can think of the worst and know that God's "best" overcomes it. Jesus conquers death with eternal life. God opens up a residence for the faithful and he dwells in their midst.

It's what John said in the prologue to his gospel, *The Word became flesh and made his dwelling among us. We have seen his glory, the glory of the one and only Son, who came from the Father, full of grace and truth.* Literally, "he pitched his tent on our campground." Now we see the end of life. We see something similar and yet different. Instead of God camping with us, we have been invited to camp with God. But what a campground! He once inhabited our "turf,"

146

but now we have an abode in his kingdom of glory, forever and ever.

Personal Reflections

Writing this book on the first three chapters of *The Revelation of Jesus Christ* gave me a richer understanding of both Jesus and the church. When I pored over the text of the first three chapters of Revelation for the umpteenth time as I prepared this manuscript, I reflected on some matters that should have been obvious just from reading the Gospels, Acts and the Epistles.

Fatherhood.

I believe I came to understand more completely that Jesus elevated the word "father." The Fourth Gospel tells how Jesus used an intimate word that a child would use to converse with his Father. The word is *"Abba,"* – Daddy! One year my wife and I vacationed at a hotel along the Dead Sea. At the beach one day we saw a child playing in the "sand" and wading in the salty water. Her father, lounging nearby, carefully watched for her safety. Every so often she would call out *"Abba"* to her daddy who watched her frolic along the shore. She wanted him to see and know everything she was doing, and obviously wanted his undivided attention and approval.

Jesus elevated the word Father to its proper perspective. Often fathers do not live up to their responsibilities. Some are putative and presumed fathers. Other fathers are irresponsible and leave mothers all the responsibilities of raising the child they sired. Many fathers are abusive. Still more are deadbeat. They accept no responsibility for the child(ren) they begat. Jesus taught his

147

disciples to speak to God as a child to an accountable father. "Our Father," he instructed them, are the words to begin their prayers. Jesus taught us about responsible fatherhood and responsible children's responses to that reality. The thought was always there in the scripture. The psalter taught it centuries before Jesus instructed us to say, "Our Father."

> *The Lord is compassionate and gracious, slow to anger, abounding in love. He will not always accuse, nor will he harbor his anger forever; he does not treat us as our sins deserve or repay us according to our iniquities. For as high as the heavens are above the earth, so great is his love for those who fear him; as far as the east is from the west, so far has he removed our transgressions from us. As a father has compassion on his children, so the Lord has compassion* [literally, "so the Lord has sensitivity in his womb"] *on those who fear him; for he knows how we are formed, he remembers that we are dust* (Psalm 103:8–14).

The concept of father-son connection is expressed throughout the New Testament. Jesus said, "*I and the Father are one,*" (8:16: see also 14:11; 17:21–23). "*Whoever has seen me has seen the Father*" (6:46), he told the people. Jesus used words identical to the words of Yahweh to connect them. God told Moses his private name. "*I am who I am,*" or "*I will be what I will be*" (Exodus 3:14). Jesus connected that truth with a series of statements in John's Gospel. "*I am* . . . *the bread*" (6:35) . . . "*I am the light*" (8:12) . . . "*I am the door*" (7:9) . . . "*I am the way, the truth and the life*" (14:6) *I am the resurrection* (11:25). And "*before Abraham was born, I am*" (John 8:58).

In *Revelation* we see an extension of the Fatherhood of God. The concept is demonstrated with the same authority of Jesus enthroned with the Father. Jesus always knew he had authority and that the Father gave it to him (Revelation 2:27; 3:5). His parting words to those who watched him ascend into heaven were clearly understood by the Lord, *"All authority (power) in heaven and on earth has been given to me"* (Matthew 28:18).

God's Wondrous Church.

Revelation provides us with a God-view of how Jesus saw his Church. Moderns have much criticism of the church. They say, "Jesus *Yes*; Church, *No!*" Certainly many churches leave much to be desired in their affirmation of faith or in their behaviours or in their misrepresentation of Jesus' gospel. Readers need to know the brighter, the better reality. Far too much is said by way of denigration to the body that Jesus loved. *"Christ loved the church and gave himself up for her to make her holy, cleansing her by the washing with water through the word, and to present her to himself as a radiant church, without stain or wrinkle or any other blemish, but holy and blameless"* (Ephesians 5:25b–27).

Bad mouthing the Church is not "on." How dare believers malign what God loves? Such denigration is undignified and dishonouring of Christ's followers. *Revelation* builds on what Paul told Ephesus. The Revelation of Jesus offers everyone a picture of a beautiful person in the form of a bride, walking down the aisle on her wedding day. Never mind what she may have been. What she is today is what counts. She is radiant as a bride should be. She has no stains, wrinkles or blemishes because God has removed them. She carries no blame, no shame. She is holy, sanctified

149

by the Almighty himself through the atoning work of Jesus upon the cross of Calvary.

God has a love affair with his people. That was true when Israel vacillated in its faith. The book of Hosea (his name means *God Saves*) tells the love story God has with people. How God loved Israel and Judah! How hard God tried to show his love for these people! God wanted Hosea to illustrate by his own life, the extent God goes to, in offering his love even to wayward wives and debased cuckolding suitors. He would seek out the lost wife and by his eternal love, attempt to woo her by his loving forgiveness.

> *"Therefore I am now going to allure her; I will lead her into the wilderness and speak tenderly to her. There I will give her back her vineyards, and will make the Valley of Achor a door of hope.*
>
> *There she will respond as in the days of her youth, as in the day she came up out of Egypt. "In that day," declares the Lord, "you will call me 'my husband'; you will no longer call me 'my master.' I will remove the names of the Baals from her lips; no longer will their names be invoked.*
>
> *In that day I will make a covenant for them with the beasts of the field, the birds in the sky and the creatures that move along the ground. Bow and sword and battle. I will abolish from the land, so that all may lie down in safety. I will betroth you to me forever; I will betroth you in righteousness and justice, in love and compassion.*
>
> *I will betroth you in faithfulness, and you will acknowledge the Lord. "In that day I will respond," declares the Lord — "I will respond to the skies, and they will respond to the earth; and*

the earth will respond to the grain, the new wine and the olive oil, and they will respond to Jezreel.

I will plant her for myself in the land; I will show my love to the one I called 'Not my loved one.' I will say to those called 'Not my people,' 'You are my people'; and they will say, 'You are my God'" (Hosea 2:14 –23).

Only when Israelites denied the Messiah he provided for them did God recognize a New Israel, the Church (Romans 9:8). Not that God stopped loving Jews! His love continues for them as Paul stated.

"I do not want you to be ignorant of this mystery, brothers and sisters, so that you may not think you are superior: Israel has experienced a hardening in part until the full number of the Gentiles has come in, and in this way all Israel will be saved. As it is written: 'The deliverer will come from Zion; he will turn godlessness away from Jacob. And this is my covenant with them when I take away their sins'" (Romans 11:25 *ff.*).

The Jews' refusal, however, allowed the Church to gain what Jews willingly lost. God was doing in the Church what Jesus taught about a servant who did not do what his master had commissioned him to do (Matthew 25:26–30). The master took from him the privilege of serving because he had not fulfilled what the master had assigned him. As Paul stated, *"It is required of stewards that they be found faithful"* (1 Corinthians 4:2). That's the way God works.

Therefore, God assigned to the Church he loved what Israel (whom he also loved and loves) did not do. God gave his beloved, redeemed, and sanctified Church a mission that Jews refused. The Church had "a story to tell to the nations," as the hymn says. Moreover, despite whatever misadventures the people of God might experience, they needed to know that their God was with them as surely as he pitched his own tent among the people of Israel in their wilderness encampments. Paul noted:

> *His intent was that now, through the church, the manifold wisdom of God should be made known to the rulers and authorities in the heavenly realms, according to his eternal purpose that he accomplished in Christ Jesus our Lord. In him and through faith in him we may approach God with freedom and confidence. I ask you, therefore, not to be discouraged because of my sufferings for you, which are your glory* (Ephesians 3:10–13).

God loved his Church so much that he saw his people as a holy temple which he could inhabit, a temple like Zion's temple in which he "allowed his name to dwell." Peter wrote:

> *As you come to him, the living Stone—rejected by human beings but chosen by God and precious to him—you also, like living stones, are being built into a spiritual house to be a holy priesthood, offering spiritual sacrifices acceptable to God through Jesus Christ. For in Scripture it says:*
>
> *"See, I lay a stone in Zion, a chosen and precious cornerstone, and the one who trusts in him will never be put to shame." Now to you who believe, this stone is precious. But to those who do not believe, "The stone the builders rejected has become the cornerstone," and, "A stone that causes people to stumble and a rock that makes them fall."*
>
> *They stumble because they disobey the message— which is also what they were destined for. But you*

are a chosen people, a royal priesthood, a holy nation, God's special possession, that you may declare the praises of him who called you out of darkness into his wonderful light. Once you were not a people, but now you are the people of God; once you had not received mercy, but now you have received mercy (1 Peter 2:4–10).

These writings of Paul and Peter elevate the Church to an unprecedented level. Pauline and Petrine letters simply prepare the reader of *The Revelation of Jesus Christ* for this incomparable God-view of the Church of Jesus Christ.

Come, I will show you the bride, the wife of the Lamb." And he carried me away in the Spirit to a mountain great and high, and showed me the Holy City, Jerusalem, coming down out of heaven from God. It shone with the glory of God, and its brilliance was like that of a very precious jewel, like a jasper, clear as crystal" (Revelation 20:9c–11) . . . *"The Spirit and the bride say, 'Come!' And let those who hear say, 'Come!' Let those who are thirsty come; and let all who wish take the free gift of the water of life"* (Revelation 22:17).

Jesus Beyond the Gospels and Epistles

Readers form images of Jesus each time they open the scriptures. No one gospel paints his portrait exactly the same. Every reading of a passage gives the reader more light and insight about Jesus. Even when all the portraits are assembled and integrated they still do an injustice to the Lord. Even his story is short-changed in the gospel accounts, as John attests. *"Jesus did many other things as well. If every one of them were written down, I suppose that even the whole world would not have room for the books that would be written"* (John 21:25). He is more than the biblical artists can portray. He is more than our evoked emotions can grasp. He is more. Period!

Readers meet Jesus first in prophetic writing. Isaiah tells of God's promise to provide One who would be a wonderful counselor, a mighty prince, and an atoning sufferer. Jeremiah tells of a new covenant, yet to come. Other prophets offer teasing bites about what Messiah will do and where he will perform his orders. Read carefully, and one sees Jesus in the first chapters of Genesis and throughout the 39 books of scripture until we arrive at Malachi, the last book in the Old Covenant. These pictures of Jesus are somewhat subtle and partially hazy. But they are there.

Mark is the first to describe Jesus. He was not a primary disciple of Jesus. So he writes from later personal experience and quotes witnesses to Jesus' words and works. His book may be placed second in the New Testament canon but he has set the template for the other gospel writers to follow.

He begins with John's announcement that Messiah was on his way. *Mark* describes John's ministry and sets the stage for Jesus' baptism and ministry. Then he tells how Jesus was tempted, called disciples and healed many who were suffering. He tells how Jesus put aside the quaint interpretations of religious leaders and having cut through the items that separated people from knowing God, lent his authority to change how humankind could relate to God. *Mark* carries the narrative through some of Jesus' teaching, through some of his ordeals, and through some of his opposition. Finally, he relates how Jesus suffered, died on a cross, was killed, buried and resurrected. Mark raises our understanding of Jesus from the pictures in the Old Testament.

Matthew builds on Mark and tells us much more about Jesus. We read of his birth, born as a king, worshipped by kings, threatened by another king. He is, however, King of the kingdom of heaven. Matthew dares not write "kingdom of God" because "God" is too sacred a word to use for the audience Matthew is addressing. Matthew uses a euphemism, "heaven," to describe Jesus' kingdom. The kingdom of heaven is where men and women permit God to rule in their hearts. Everything in Matthew's gospel acknowledges the Sovereignty of God and how Jesus' words and works are a part of that.

Luke likewise uses Mark's writing to tell still more about Jesus. His audience is different and he has no compunction about using "kingdom of God" to describe the realm about which Jesus is teaching. His theme is different, of course. He starts by placing Jesus' birth in the rule of Tiberius Caesar. His birth narrative sets the stage for Luke's emphasis on the marginalized of society. Jesus is born in a stable. Those first to adore him are the poorest of the poor, non-observant sheep keepers. Jesus announces his intentions to fulfill the prophecy of Isaiah by liberating the people on the edges of life who are left out of life's mainstream by poverty, self-denigration, disease or ostricization.

Read Luke and you read about real poverty. Luke recounts many stories about eating, something which with his audience would easily identify because they could not afford food. He tells how Jesus relates to people who lose things, or have unexpected visitors in the middle of the night, or who agonize over a son who strays from a God-rule. Luke shows Jesus as liberator of the marginalized and friend of the poor. Like the other Gospels, Luke tells of Jesus' suffering, death, burial and resurrection.

John chooses to explain Jesus as the "Word." Jesus is God's love-message to humankind. He also is the messenger. It is a message of love, not just for a Semite segment of society but also for the entire world. *"For God so loved the world that he gave his one and only Son, that whoever believes in him shall not perish but have eternal life. For God did not send his Son into the world to condemn the world, but to save the world through him"* (John 3:16, 17). John presents Jesus as fully human, fully divine. To see Jesus is to see exactly what God is like, loving, caring, healing, redemptive, and authoritative. Of course, Jesus is much more than that – as is God.

The Epistles (letters) add to the portrait of the Lord by filling in much more about Jesus than the Gospel narratives tell a reader. The narrative of Jesus' life, ministry, death and resurrection morphs into more developed explanations of who Jesus is in terms of God's destiny for the world. The reader is moved into seeing Jesus as the centre of living, the focus of all history, the measure of all love, the apex of God's ultimate plan for the cosmos.

When one reads *Romans* one reads of the redemptive work carried out by God's Messiah. This is Israel completed. Paul explains what Jesus told his listeners at a communion table, that after he left them he would send his Spirit. Indeed, the Holy Spirit has come to convict sinful people of their need to know and accept God's forgiveness, to receive his grace and mercy. Jesus is righteous, the world is sinful. Jesus answers this deficit in the world by making righteous those who receive God's grace and express their faith in Jesus' expiation on the cross. But it cannot be a nominal expression of faith. It must be vocal and heart-felt (Romans 10:9).

That Jesus sent his Holy Spirit to Christians in Corinth is also a theme of the two letters from Paul. Corinthians didn't quite get it, so Paul explained that the love of Jesus Christ is so deep and so wide that it is the greatest asset God can give people. Christ's love exceeds division, breaches quarrels and supersedes human aspirations. His love heals human fractures and his sovereignty orders our daily living. He wanted Corinth to know how he felt about Christ: *"we make it our goal to please him"* (2:5:9). Paul wanted to put a smile on his Lord's face!

Galatians, a letter sent by Paul attempted to allay the understanding by some Jews that non-Jews may receive Christ as Saviour but first they must obey the various Jewish legal requirements of ritual purifications – washings, Sabbath-keeping, circumcision and renunciation of eating prohibited foods, i.e., pork. Not so, wrote Paul. Believers do not earn salvation by performance but by faith. Even faith is not earned but a gift of grace from the Eternal grace-giver. Grace and faith level all believers to have no claim on privilege. Grace, whose source is Jesus, equals everyone by elevating everyone by adoption as God's children and a "faith-descendant" of Abraham. *"Now that faith has come, wrote Paul,"we are no longer under the supervision of the law"* (Galatians 3:25).

Paul addressed some similar situations in Ephesus. In *Ephesians*, Jesus is explained as the greatest shalom, who made peace between Jews and non-Jews. Jesus is the gift benefactor, the empowerer who provides both people and spiritual talents for his holy Church.

In one metaphor, Paul portrays Jesus as a victorious general who has returned in a Roman-like triumph to his base to receive the accolades of his people. Like the Roman general's reception celebrating a triumph, the crowds shower him with perfumed petals (Roman soldiers got very sweaty!) to provide a friendly fragrance. Trailing behind his entourage, were the chained captives he brought with him. They were symbols of his victory. Christ's presence is sweet and fragrant. He endows his people with appropriate aids to augment his governance. He distributed a variety of gifts to those who arrived to welcome him home as victor.

To Philippi, Paul wrote about "joy in Jesus." Jesus is among us as a servant leader. Paul urged his friends to put aside their differences and find their purpose for life in Christ. He stressed the descent of Jesus to the human condition and the glory of Jesus in the eyes of the Father. In *Philippians*, chapter two, Paul linked that descent and elevation of the Lord to what the Fourth Gospel also tells readers in the first 18 verses of *John*. Both John and Paul use a poetic form to state this case.

Christians in Colossae needed a vision of Jesus beyond their puny grasp of spiritual reality. Paul described Christ Jesus as the Creator and synthesizer of creation (1:17). He used an image similar to a captain charioteer holding all the reins, spurring his horses, commanding them to the right or left, urging them on to catch the opposition.

158

Christians, according to Paul in *Colossians*, must forsake allegiances to anyone other than Christ himself. Worshipping Christ's messengers is not "on."

In watershed words to the Colossian believers as noted earlier, Paul directs them to absorb themselves in Christ. *"So then, just as you received Christ Jesus as Lord, continue to live your lives in him, rooted and built up in him, strengthened in the faith as you were taught, and overflowing with thankfulness"* Colossians 2:6, 7).

The book of *Hebrews* relegates Christ to the realm of majesty and superiority. *"(God's) Son is the radiance of God's glory and the exact representation of his being, sustaining all things by his powerful word. After he had provided purification for sins, he sat down at the right hand of the Majesty in heaven"* (Hebrews 1:3). Christ is better than the angels, better than Moses and Abraham. Jesus is better than all priests because he is the perfect, sinless priest and by his sinlessness, Jesus is the perfect offering sacrifice for the sins of humankind. He is better than the law because the law bows down to him.

The three letters of John reminded the Church that love is perfected in Jesus Christ. Temples to the love gods and goddess abounded in the Graeco-Roman world, as they had in Phrygia, ancient Egypt and Canaan. Eros, the Greek god of love provided the world with "eroticism." Christ, provided *agape* love. That was unconditional love, without strings attached, self-giving without seeking a reward. Erotic love is not wrong, but it can never be the object of worship in itself. Christ illustrated the kind of love that could be venerated. Love is incarnated in Jesus Christ.

The letters of *Peter* offer believers a view of Christ as the strength-giver, whose word offers self-worth to his followers. How important that was to apprehensive believers who knew that the Emperor's justice was right around the corner! Christians had royal blood running through their veins, no matter their derision of Caesar by his claim of divinity. King Jesus has made them what they are. Their purpose, therefore, despite Caesar's edicts demanding his people's submission, is to tell of Sovereign Jesus' victories over sin and death.

> *You are a chosen people, a royal priesthood, a holy nation, God's special possession, that you may declare the praises of him who called you out of darkness into his wonderful light. Once you were not a people, but now you are the people of God; once you had not received mercy, but now you have received mercy* (1Peter 2:9. 10).

All the images of Jesus Christ as seen through the Gospels and the Letters, coalesce in *Revelation*. All the foregoing images contribute to our perception of Jesus, but *Revelation* kneads them together and melds them into a final appraisal of who Jesus is.

This book has not dealt with chapters four to the end, nor was that its purpose. The chapters following the word of the Holy Spirit to the churches, is wrought with viewing the agony of Christ battling the enemy of God's love, grace, mercy and forgiveness. It is a painful battle to watch from the sidelines. Praise God we had a warrior who did it for us! Evil is as macabre, black and ugly as the contest describes.

Revelation completes the perceptions we see of Jesus Christ in the earlier chapters of the New Testament. Christ emerges from it all as supreme. *Revelation* shows him as victor over all forces of evil, corruption and death. Jesus is Majesty. He is Sovereign. He is Approved by the Father. He is Judge. He is Head of the Family who welcomes his redeemed children, the trophies of his grace, into the full, uninhibited presence of his Father.